MY FOUR
Hollywood
HUSBANDS

JOYCE BULIFANT

Song lyrics quoted—"Someone to Watch Over Me" by George Gershwin; "I Ain't Down Yet" by Meredith Willson

All photos and images are from the private collection of Ms. Bulifant. Several of these are decades-old newspaper clippings, and some have lost their original vibrancy.

Publishing Consultant: David Wogahn, DavidWogahn.com
Cover design by Ana Agüero

Tilton Bass Publishing
Palm Springs, CA
tiltonbass@icloud.com

First Edition
Printed in the United States of America

To
Charlie, Mary, John,
Brian, Liane, Billy, Robert, Rebecca,
Chris and Dana

And my loving husband, Roger

Don't let your past rob your future.

Each new day is a chance
to make a new beginning.
Count your blessings,
live with gratitude
and love with all your heart!

Contents

Introduction

This is a book about love, a lasting love that is woven through the fabric of the world of entertainment, alcoholism, codependency and family.

It's about truth… my truth… my perspective.

It is my hope that everyone reading this love story will understand the hurt the alcoholic and the codependent cause others and—most important—the harm that children endure.

It is also my hope that anyone caught in the web of addiction will understand that it's possible to detach with love and go on with life.

First you learn. Perhaps mistakes will follow. But if you keep learning and trying, there can be a happy ending.

ONE

The Frog Prince and the Queen

Mother and her beau Charles drove me from scary New York City to the serene countryside of Bucks County, Pennsylvania. After passing through the charming town of New Hope, we traveled up a hill lined with oak trees and arrived at a beautiful farm house and barn that had become Solebury, a coed boarding school. A blue and white sign swung gently at the entrance. This sign marked not only the entrance to a wonderful school, but the entrance to a whole new life for me. It was there that I met James MacArthur.

He was stocky, with sensitive blue eyes and sandy-colored, curly hair. I heard that his mother, Helen Hayes, was a famous Broadway actress, but I only knew about movie stars, so her name didn't mean much to me.

When Miss Hayes arrived at school with her sullen, but wickedly good-looking son, I was invited to join them at lunch because I was in the drama club. I expected Miss Hayes to arrive wearing dark sunglasses, carrying a cigarette holder and draped in a mink coat. Instead, Mrs. MacArthur looked rather ordinary—not glamorous, not sophisticated—but like any other mother. I was much more fascinated with her son. Jimmy was fourteen and would be in my class.

It didn't take me long, however, to realize that Jimmy was a perfect jerk, sometimes perfect and sometimes a jerk.

Our English teacher was a mousy, soft-spoken young woman. Jim, wanting to endear himself to his new classmates, decided to pull a mean-spirited prank on her. When she tried to stand and write on the blackboard, she found she was stuck to her chair. Jimmy had put glue on her seat! The teacher kept trying to pull herself up. When she finally freed herself from the sticky mess, she ran from the classroom in tears.

Stunned with rage toward the perpetrator, I looked over at Jimmy, who was at his desk, writing feverishly. When he finished, he passed around a note of apology for each of us to sign. Everyone's signature appeared on the note, save one—Jimmy MacArthur's.

One of his tricks was offering candy his mom had sent him. Just as I reached for a piece, he'd pull the box away. I decided Jimmy MacArthur was too immature for me. After all, I was dating an upper classman, Michael Laine, who was sixteen, popular and president of his class. He had a crewcut, and when he dressed up he wore bow ties. As Mike's girlfriend, I became the envy of the girls in my class and his.

*

I had always been in school plays, from my earliest days. Although I could barely read, my parts had more meaning for me than the words in textbooks, and I was motivated to memorize my lines. My dyslexia, unrecognized until many years later, meant that I was a very slow reader. I mispronounced many words, and my spelling was a disaster. But when the Drama Club announced tryouts for the play "The Birthday of the Infanta," I asked a teacher for help with some of the words. Then I went to my room and studied way past lights out, with a flashlight under the sheets. I said the lines over and over again and before I knew it, the sun was up. I desperately wanted the role of the court jester, the one who gives the moon to the princess for her birthday. That afternoon, standing in the hall of the old gym waiting my turn to try out, I heard the others read for the role. It seemed they recited without heart, just reading lines. I told myself, "I will be the court jester the minute I walk onto the gym floor."

The edges of the playbook were wet with perspiration from my nervous hands, but I had memorized every word. When I heard my name, my knees almost buckled, I dropped my playbook, picked it up, and took a deep breath before I walked in to face the drama coach, who was seated at a table. There was a pause—silence—and then I did a somersault, leaped up, and right before her eyes became the jester! I got the part.

There was no turning back. Pretending to be a character, having an audience of parents, teachers and classmates who laughed and applauded made me feel accepted. I became involved in some capacity in every production. More than anything else, this helped me learn to read. I was no longer just seeing black letters on a white page, but words that were spoken in sadness or happiness, along with gestures that illustrated the words and told a story.

That winter, I was in "A Christmas Carol." A producer, Peter Flannoy, who was a friend of the Laine family, saw me in the play and asked if I would like to work as an apprentice in his professional summer stock theater, the Grove Theatre. At fourteen, I would be the youngest person on the staff; the other apprentices were just out of college. He offered to have me stay with him and his mother. Amazingly, Mother agreed that it was a wonderful opportunity.

The Grove Theatre, where young actors like Kirk Douglas got their start, was located on Lake Nuangola in the mountains near Wilkes-Barre, Pennsylvania. (Years later, when I worked with Kirk, we laughed about our auspicious debuts!) I did all the dirty work, including cleaning the toilets. But who cared? I was in the theater! I swept the stage, mixed paint for the sets, cleaned the paint buckets, learned how to work the light board, and brought coffee to the weary actors who rehearsed a new play each week.

What wonderful, creative actors they were! With my plumber's stick in hand, I would stand at the back of the darkened theater,

Confidence does it

mesmerized, watching rehearsals. Each week we would have a visiting star. Some were from the old silent films. I did bit parts, usually playing the maid or the young girl. The first play I did at The Grove was "Foolish Notion." On opening night as I applied my makeup, my mouth was dry and my hands were shaking. I stared at the paneled wall where someone had carved "Confidence Does It."

I summoned up all the confidence I could. That calmed me down until the curtain opened. I took center stage, singing, "Poor Wandering One," my heart beating so hard I could see the ruffles on my dress shaking.

The role I became most infamous for, however, was that of costume and prop mistress during a play with visiting actor Edward Everett Horton. He was a well-known character actor and the voice of the cartoon, "Fractured Flickers." He asked me to iron the silk pajamas he wore in the play. I burned an iron-sized hole right in the seat of his pants (it's difficult to iron silk, especially on a collapsible ironing board). Besides doing props for Mr. Horton's production, I was also cast as a young maid in the play. Before the show, I had to make the "wine," which was really water with red food coloring.

Before one Sunday matinee, Mr. Horton asked me to refrigerate the liquid. He complained that by the time he made a toast at the end of the play, he was choking down flies! I went to the theater early to sweep the stage and get the props ready. This time when I went to make the wine, I couldn't find the box of food coloring. I panicked and ran to the prop house to see if I could find a box there. I rummaged through the shelves and suddenly a giant moose head fell on me, along with a box of grape Jell-O. Oh joy! If I put a pinch of grape Jell-O in water, it would look like wine. I mixed a pinch of grape Jell-O with water and filled each glass, which I put in the refrigerator.

At the end of the play I came on stage with the tray of wine glasses. Everyone took a glass. Mr. Horton made a toast. The gentlemen clinked glasses and raised the glasses to their lips. A big glob of Jell-O hit them right in the face! Were they ever startled! Mr. Horton was furious with me. After the show, he tied me to a tree in front of the theater, just to teach me a lesson.

Notwithstanding these embarrassing episodes, I loved acting. In addition to doing summer stock, over the next few years at school I performed in every play I could.

✳

The winter I was sixteen, during a break from classes, Mike asked me to take a walk with him. Under the leafless branches of the willow tree by the frozen pond, he told me he was going to college in the fall. After three years of dating, summer trips with his family to Nantucket, spring walks along the Delaware canal, and stolen kisses after dances in the gym, he wanted to break up. I didn't know what to say. I couldn't look at him. I stood alone under the willow tree and watched him walk away. The pain was intense and familiar, the same pain I had felt as a young girl when my mother told me my father was gone.

One morning a teacher announced, "Today is fall holiday. There will be a picnic at Bowman's Tower on the Delaware River, and tonight the school bus will take you to a movie. Have a great holiday!" I was delighted, but Mike had broken my heart and I had no date for the movies. Young sweethearts walked hand in hand to the buses. Bucks Country in the fall is truly the most spectacular of God's paintings. The bus traveled through the brightly-colored countryside along the Delaware River. At the picnic I quietly took in the crisp, fresh smell of autumn. Later, across the field by an old mill, I saw Jimmy MacArthur, who seemed to be waving in my direction. I looked around to see if he might be waving to someone else, but he continued to wave and ran toward me.

"Listen, I'm sorry about you and Mike and everything. I mean I never liked you much, but you know, I really felt sorry for you." He looked handsome in a navy turtleneck sweater, with his curly hair

Jimmy

shining in the setting sun. "Would you go to the movies with me tonight?"

I was dumbstruck.

Soon after our first date, I told Jimmy if he wanted to keep dating me, he'd have to join the drama club. He did, and I became his steady date. That summer he performed with his famous mother in summer stock and parked cars at the Falmouth Playhouse in Cape Cod.

One weekend, Jimmy invited me to his home in Nyack, in upstate New York. My mother gave me permission and a door opened to a whole new world.

Jimmy's father, playwright Charles MacArthur, named their home "Pretty Penny" because he said that's what it cost, a pretty penny! It was a beautiful white, three-story Victorian with green shutters overlooking the Hudson River. Among the many rooms was a music room with a piano that Mrs. MacArthur proudly said Gershwin had played.

Jim's home in Nyack

Each room had a coal-burning fireplace and large windows draped in embroidered organdy for summer, and in the winter, rose-print chintz curtains. The main living room opened out onto a large porch. Steps circling left and right led from the porch down to a sloping lawn with four terraces. The first terrace was decorated with wrought-iron lawn furniture framed by two gigantic oak trees. Brick stairs led to the next level and a pond filled with water lilies, enough to grace a Monet painting. Brick walkways circled the pond leading to Mrs. MacArthur's fragrant, lovingly-tended rose gardens. Grass steps led to the next level, where dogwood trees framed a swimming pool and cabana. Below was a clay tennis court and beyond that, a rolling lawn with apple trees sloped down to the banks of the Hudson. To the left of the orchard was a gardener's hut, perfect for two sixteen-year-olds to hide, steal kisses, and tell each other their dreams.

When we arrived at Pretty Penny, Jimmy led me through the front door of his stately home and into the foyer. I was more than impressed—I was terrified! Maybe Jim's mother was going to be very different from the woman I had met at school two years ago, a sweet motherly type. Maybe now the real person, the "Actress" would appear, grand and intimidating.

I followed Jimmy up a circular stairwell. Mrs. MacArthur, as I called her for the first visit, had played Queen Victoria on Broadway to much acclaim, and on the wall next to the staircase were etchings of Queen Victoria's ladies-in-waiting. At the top of the stairs, Jimmy took me down a long hallway. My heart was in my throat and refused to go back where it belonged. What would I find at the end of this hallway, a Queen sitting on her throne?

Jim opened a heavy wooden door. I saw a large white sheet floating in the air. It drifted down to reveal Mrs. MacArthur, who was making her husband's bed. Her hair was tied in a babushka, and her dress was covered with an apron. She smiled the warmest, most welcoming smile and asked me, "Do you like strawberry shortcake? Would that be all right for dessert tonight?"

It was my favorite dessert. I answered a resounding, "Yes, that would be lovely."

Thus began one of the most loving and complicated relationships I would ever know.

TWO

Traveling with the Queen

D inner in Nyack took place at a large gray wooden table. There were clouds painted on the ceiling and the tall dining room windows looked out at magnificent large trees. Jim's Mom told me that once during a raging storm, she stood by the windows and yelled, "Hold fast my trees!" She could be quite dramatic.

I was sorry to learn that Jimmy's sister, Mary, had died from polio when she was only nineteen. A beautiful portrait of her in a burgundy dress hung over a Victorian love seat covered in the same color as her dress. A bouquet of pink roses sat on a small table near her portrait.

After dinner, Charlie MacArthur sat by the coal-burning fireplace in an overstuffed velvet chair. A standard poodle named Nappy, short for Napoleon, reclined by his side.

"So you want to be an actress?" he asked me, rather impishly.

"Yes, sir."

He tried to look stern. "Well, you have to be in forty flops before you're a star!"

Mr. MacArthur was a bit of a jokester. I liked him right away.

I wondered if Mrs. MacArthur had been in forty flops.

I was sixteen years old and very impressed with the beautiful home on the Hudson River. It was to become my first real home. Jim's Mom kept inviting me from school on weekends and holidays. Often Mother and Charles were invited too. Mother seemed very pleased that I spent so much time in Nyack; I guess it gave her time to be with Charles.

The winter of my seventeenth year, Jimmy took me to see his mother in a Broadway play, "What Every Women Knows." I was very nervous for her. To me she was simply "Jim's Mom." I had never seen her act. I, of course, knew all about acting (at least I thought I did). We sat on the aisle in the third row, and Jimmy held my hand. The curtain rose. I stopped breathing—I was so nervous for her. She was sitting on a sofa, center stage, knitting. Peering out into the audience she found Jimmy and me and gave a wink in our direction. Oh no!!! She's not in character. She's not concentrating!! Poor Jimmy, he's going to be so embarrassed. I squeezed his hand hard. Then as the actors started their dialogue, I became so engrossed in the play that "Jim's Mom" had absolutely become the character in the play.

After the performance, Jimmy took me backstage. In her dressing room was the famous acting pair, Alfred Lunt and Lynn Fontaine. Sir Lawrence Olivier was there, along with the famous silent screen actress, Lillian Gish. They were all praising her performance, beginning each sentence with "Darling!" and "My dear!" wrapped around many other adjectives of approval. I said, "Excuse me" as I walked through the royalty of American Theater towards Helen Hayes. I hugged her and said, "You know what?... You were good!"

NEW YORK TIMES, SUNDAY, MAY 15, 1955.   DRAMA—SCREEN

A REIGNING STAR IN HER PORTRAYALS OF SOME ROYAL LADIES

Helen Hayes in three of four scenes from a program called "Gentlemen, the Queen," which will play in Ann Arbor, Mich., for a week starting tomorrow. Miss Hayes will portray Mary of Scotland, at left; Victoria, center; Catherine the Great, right, and Lady Macbeth. The production was presented for one performance last week at the Solebury School, New Hope, Pa., and may be done on the strawhat circuit in late summer.

The following spring, Helen Hayes came to Solebury to help raise money for our school. She did "An Evening of Queens," performing scenes from each of the plays in which she'd portrayed royalty. I was asked to play her lady-in-waiting in the scene in which she was Catherine the Great.

During the scene, as she stood and delivered her monologue, I was to button the little pearl buttons on her salmon-colored cloak and its long train. I had to work quickly and silently.

The night of the show, I finished the last button in time for her to turn and make her dramatic exit, but she couldn't move! She turned in my direction and I got a very dirty look from the First Lady of the American Theatre. I didn't understand why. Had I buttoned her buttons incorrectly, were they crooked? Suddenly she yanked her train and I went ass over teacups! She couldn't move because I was standing on her train!

That same night, Jimmy was in a scene as she portrayed Queen Victoria. Inside her cheeks she had placed Vaseline-soaked cotton to make them look chubby like the elderly ruler. Jim played the queen's aide, who pushed her in a wheelchair. This was the famous scene in which Queen Victoria gives her most moving, stirring speech to the crowds at her Diamond Jubilee. Just before her most important line, she paused for dramatic effect. Jim thought she was finished and started wheeling her off the stage. At that point, the old Queen dug her heels into the stage floor, making skid marks! Only then did Jimmy get the cue to wheel her back around, facing the audience, so that she could finish her line. For a few hours after the performance, Jimmy and I steered clear of his famous mother.

Our junior year, Jim won the Harvard Book Award, given to an academically outstanding student. I was so proud of him. That's also the year when we were given our class rings. Jimmy gave me his ring, and I wore it proudly on a gold chain around my neck, happy to be his steady girlfriend.

That summer, Jimmy was asked to audition for a television show called "Climax" in the role of a disturbed young boy from a Beverly Hills family. Jimmy won the role and went to Los Angeles to film the show. I watched the TV show from Pennsylvania, where I was doing my third year in summer stock. He was perfect in the part and did a great job.

I continued having terrible difficulties with my schoolwork, barely passing. It wasn't until I was in my forties that I found out I was dyslexic, a little-known condition in those days. I struggled at night, studying in the bathtub with a flashlight long after lights out. Even now, I have nightmares about failing to graduate. My senior year was much easier. I took chorus, art, drama, and physiology. I memorized human anatomy, but don't ask me the name of one bone in our bodies today!

Two months before graduation, Jimmy was called from class and told his father had died. A car was waiting to take him to Nyack. Poor

Jimmy, I felt so sad for him. He loved his father so much and was very close to him. Although his father had been in ill health for some time, it was still a shock. My heart went out to Mrs. MacArthur, who adored her Charlie. She had lost a daughter and now her husband.

My mother and Charles took me to the funeral service at Campbell's in New York City. Afterwards we drove to Nyack to be with Jimmy. We arrived to find a crowded living room. Spotting Jimmy through the crowd, I went straight to him and put my arms around him. His eyes were red and he was very pale in his black suit.

"Mom said she wants to see you. She's upstairs in bed. I'll take you up there."

Jimmy took me into his mother's room and left me alone with her. She motioned for me to sit on her bed. Taking my hands in hers, she said, "I'm so glad you came. Here I am in bed—it seems I take to my bed with a cold whenever tragedy knocks on my heart."

I reached over and hugged her. Lying in bed under the covers, she looked so small and frail. My heart ached for her.

A week later Jimmy and I were back in school. There was more sadness now than ever in Jimmy's blue eyes. A few weeks later, right before our senior prom, I was called from my classroom to answer a phone call in the office. My mother, her voice quivering, told me her mother had passed away that morning. Muz, my wonderful grandmother, was only fifty-six when a blood clot went to her heart and she was taken from us.

Our senior year, Jimmy was going to star in the school production of "Charley's Aunt." But he was still behaving badly, and they weren't going to let him do the play. He was a troubled young man, always getting into mischief at school. I was forever going to the headmaster and asking him to give Jim another chance. Jimmy had a mean streak.

He picked on the underdog, putting people down with demeaning remarks and mean-spirited pranks, which seemed to give him pleasure.

I often wondered if this need to pick on the underdog was because Jimmy was adopted, or was there some darker shadow? Perhaps Jimmy had the need to feel superior to overcome an inferiority complex? There were rumors that his father, an alcoholic and a notorious womanizer, was really his biological father. People had speculated about who his birth mother was. Ruth Gordon and Bea Lillie, two famous actresses, were mentioned.

I thought Jimmy did mean things because he was unhappy. I wanted to make him happy because I felt he was a good person underneath his facade of meanness. Maybe I saw a lost child, like me. (This, I learned much later, was a mistake. I don't think you can ever make another person happy or feel loved. It is up to that person to decide if they WANT to be happy. It was a mistake I was to make many times.)

Our Senior Prom

It rained on our graduation day. Instead of gathering outside under the old elm tree, we graduated in the gym. Jimmy and I led the procession to "Pomp and Circumstance." I wore a white organdy dress with lace ruffles and carried a nosegay of white daisies and blue cornflowers, our school colors. Mother's beau Charles, the largest wholesale florist in the world, had arranged the flowers for the ceremony. I was happy not to disappoint him and Mother. I made it! I graduated.

After previously attending fifteen other schools, Solebury was a saving grace for me. I was there for six years, from seventh through twelfth grade. Not only that, but because my classes were so easy during senior year—surprise!—I graduated with honors!

There was more good news. The television show that Jimmy had done was going to be made into a motion picture, "The Young Stranger," and he would play the role he had created for television. Jimmy received a shiny black Thunderbird as a graduation present from his mother. He and Footie Glenn, his best friend, planned to drive across country to Hollywood. (Footie's real name was Phil, but his baby sister couldn't pronounce it correctly. It came out Footie, and Footie he remained.) I always liked Footie. He was from a large Catholic family that lived across the street from Jimmy in Nyack. Footie was a real stand-up guy, no frills, just a good person. Kenny Cromwell, a school friend, was going with them. They were thrilled to be going to Hollywood. "Jim's Mom," as I called her, would follow behind in her Lincoln Town Car, driven by her chauffeur. She invited me to go with her to follow Jimmy cross-country. My mother said I could go. I was so excited!

It was wonderful seeing the country with Helen. She was such fun, knowledgeable and inquisitive about everything. We saw Mt. Rushmore, Yellowstone National Park, and the Dakotas. Along the way we stopped at motels and ate great regional food. Jim and I sneaked around for stolen kisses.

Still, this was a sad time for Helen, having just lost her husband. One day, while we were driving through the amber waves of grain, giant raindrops started to pelt the windshield and tears fell gently on her cheeks. As we drove along, she sang softly.

"There's a someone I'm longing to see
I hope that he
turns out to be
someone to watch over me."

I reached over and took her hand as we rode silently through the rain.

On our way to Hollywood we stopped in San Francisco just for fun. What a beautiful city! We went to the Purple Onion, where Mort Sahl was appearing, and had a grand time. Then we traveled down the jagged California coast to Hollywood, where we stayed at the Chateau Marmont. Our room overlooked the famous Sunset Boulevard. A two-story high cowgirl, advertising beer, turned round and round outside our window. WOW! HOLLYWOOD!

On a movie set in Hollywood with Footie, Kenny,
Helen, a producer, and Michael Rennie

While Jimmy was busy at the studio, his mother took me to visit one of her dearest friends, Joan Crawford. When Miss Crawford opened the door, I thought she was the housekeeper. She had on seersucker shorts, her hair tied in a bandanna, and in her hand, she held a mop. This was a movie star?

Within moments of being ushered into her beautiful home, she led me by the hand up the grand staircase. In her glamorous mirrored bathroom, she opened a closet door to reveal hundreds of shoes! I really didn't know what reaction was expected of me. I turned to Helen for a clue, but she looked as puzzled as I did.

The whole of Hollywood turned out to welcome Helen Hayes and her son, James MacArthur, at a party at Romanoff's. It was as if I had walked into a movie magazine. Gloria and Jimmy Stewart, Ginger Rogers, and Hedda Hopper, the famous Hollywood gossip

reporter, were just a few of the famous gathered there. Kenny, Footie and I were awestruck! I wore my graduation dress with a red satin belt at the waist, pearls, and of course, little white cotton gloves. I must have looked like Alice in Wonderland among the shimmering gowns and jewels of Hollywood's royalty.

Alice in Wonderland

Footie asked me what I'd like to drink. I asked for some of that good California orange juice. The press were very busy taking pictures of Jim, Helen Hayes, and all the other Hollywood notables. I wandered around and noticed an elderly lady sitting alone. Crossing the room carefully, so as not to spill my orange juice, I went over to talk with her. For some reason, balancing my juice had become difficult. In fact, walking a straight line was difficult as well. I literally plopped myself down next to the sweet lady. Slurring, I asked her if she was having a nice time and did she attend many parties like this, or was this her first?

On the way back to the hotel, Helen informed me that the sweet little old lady was Pearl Mesta, internationally known as the "Hostess with the Mostest." Her parties for the famous were the basis for the musical "Call Me Madam." I also found out that the California oranges had vodka in them! That was my introduction to the wicked ways of Hollywood.

When I came home from Hollywood, the church janitor and I were the only witnesses to Mother's marriage to Charles. Their marriage took place in the chapel of the Methodist Church on Park Avenue. It was a perfect union between two people who had been in love for many years. After the ceremony, we went to the Rendezvous Room at the Plaza Hotel, just the three of us, for dinner and dancing. My mother looked beautiful and radiant, and my new dad looked so handsome. They danced round and round the dance floor, unaware of any other person in the room. Their two souls had become one and they were lost in the magic of the transformation.

Wedding day, Mother and Dad (Charles)

Mother and Dad were now living in a picturesque stone farmhouse in Bucks County, built in 1725, where Dad was able to grow his flowers and take them to his Philadelphia store. He planted over two thousand hybrid peonies and enjoyed tending to them. Wearing a straw hat and smoking a corncob pipe, he rode his green and yellow tractor through the fields. Mother would shout from the kitchen door across the green lawn, past the weeping willow tree and the old well, "Charles, sweetheart! Time for dinner, sweetheart, the guests are here." But she was seldom heard above the chugging sounds of his little tractor. Mother understood how he enjoyed tending to the flowers and she loved him even more.

One day Dad came back from the store in Philadelphia earlier than usual. When Mother came home from shopping, she walked into their bedroom and found their bed covered with red roses. Standing by the side of the bed, Dad said, "I always promised you a bed of roses."

*

In 1956 in New York City, I was attending The American Academy of Dramatic Arts, while in Boston, Jimmy was in his first year at Harvard. I lived in a boarding house in the East 60s for young ladies. It was named, of all things, "The Phoebe Warren House." It sounded to me like a house of ill repute! On weekends I visited Jimmy as often as possible at Harvard. I remember how embarrassed he was at the annual Harvard-Yale football game. His film, "The Young Stranger," was opening in Cambridge. In the Harvard Stadium as we watched the game, a small plane flew overhead, trailing a banner that read, "See Harvard's James MacArthur in THE YOUNG STRANGER." Jimmy was so mortified, he tried to cover his head with the hood of his jacket, like a turtle retreating into its shell. Shortly after that, Helen invited me to stay with her at The Ritz in Boston and, of course, to see Jimmy. She was in an out-of-town tryout of "Time Remembered," a play with Richard Burton and Susan Strasberg. After the performance, we went to Lee Strasberg's hotel room, where he regaled us with stories about his adventures in the Yiddish theater. I sat enraptured, listening to the famous acting coach recount his early experiences in theater. Every week they performed a different play, and several were period plays. When the actors weren't in a scene, they would throw off their heavy cloaks, take off their wigs, hang them on hooks behind a table, and get in a few hands of cards until they heard their cue. At that point they would grab their cloaks and wigs and make their entrance.

Lee said he was playing hearts one night when he heard his cue. He hurriedly grabbed a cloak and wig and rushed on stage. As he entered, the actors gave him a horrified look—they were doing a Yiddish play that week, all in modern dress, save Lee. He had grabbed a Chinese robe and put on a wig with a long pigtail. Realizing his predicament, he announced, "I may look like a Chinaman, but I'm a Jew in my heart." Then he went on with the show!

After a late evening of more theater stories, Jimmy, Helen and I went to her room at the Ritz. The suite consisted of a sitting room and twin beds in the bedroom that she and I shared. After she went to bed, Jimmy and I lay down side by side on the sofa to watch TV. Jimmy was drinking beer, surrounded by several empty cans on the floor. After a while, Helen entered, exploding into an Irish rage, the likes of which I had never seen. Such rage, emanating from this gentle person that I had grown to love! I didn't know what to think. When she yelled at Jim to leave, he fled in a panic.

She retreated to the bedroom, carrying on about Jimmy and his drinking and how she should send him back to his drunken mother in Los Angeles. I didn't know what she was talking about, and I didn't know what to do. I silently and quickly undressed, put on my night-gown, and got into bed. I was confused and very distressed. It seemed that I had heard something I shouldn't have. But this wasn't to be the last of her temper and resentment toward her son.

Jimmy had told me he was adopted when he was six months old, but no one told him. He read it in the newspaper when he was seven years old. Jimmy explained that his father had seen him in a foundling home and picked him out of all the babies to adopt. Jim went on to say that he must have been from a very wealthy family because he was dressed in silk and lace. I always thought it was a sweet story that his father, Pop, had probably made up. But Jimmy really seemed to believe it. Maybe he needed to.

Jimmy also said that Pop had always been faithful, never played around. I don't know why he felt that was important for me to know. I had heard that Charlie MacArthur had a serious drinking problem and was quite a womanizer.

The next morning at the Ritz, Helen told me that during the run of the play interesting things were happening backstage. There was a lot of intrigue between the cast members, and Susan Strasberg was having an affair with Richard Burton. One day Susan asked Helen to speak to Richard, whom Susan felt was stealing her laugh at the end of the second act. Helen suggested that since Susan was closer to Richard than she was, perhaps she should speak with him directly.

That afternoon, between the matinee and evening performances, Helen, as usual, had a meal sent to her dressing room before taking a nap. She would play music on the radio so she wouldn't hear Susan and Richard in the next dressing room. But today she was curious to hear how Susan would handle getting her laugh at the end of act two. So instead of turning on the radio, she put a glass up to the wall and listened. Richard entered Susan's room. "Hello, darling."

"Hello, my sweetheart. Could we speak a moment about the second act?" Giggling noises and sweet sounds. "No, Richard, darling, really. In the second act when... oh, Richard, no, not now, my love, wait a minute. Oh, Richard, Oh!"

Helen said, "It was the first time I ever literally heard someone get screwed out of a laugh!"

✳

During my last year at the American Academy of Dramatic Arts—I don't remember exactly how this happened—I was invited to audition for a television show, "Name That Tune." George DeWitt was master of ceremonies, and Ammident Toothpaste was the sponsor.

In a large room, a heavyset lady at the piano hammered out one hundred tunes. I was given a sheet of paper numbered from 1 to 100. I was to write down the name of each song she played. I knew just about every song—I would be a contestant!

For the show, which was live rather than prerecorded, all the contestants had to wear sneakers. When a song was played, if we knew what it was, we had to run as fast as we could, to be the first to pull the cord of a bell. Then, *Name That Tune*. The night I was on, as soon as the orchestra started playing, I immediately knew the song and took off like a bat out of hell. I yanked the cord so hard, I pulled the bell down, and the momentum caused me to slide into the pile of Ammident Toothpaste on display in front of the host. I was lying on the studio floor covered in boxes of Ammident Toothpaste with the cord of the bell still in my hand. But I knew the song!

Next came the lightning round. I had to answer as many songs as I could in a short time. I was so excited. The clock ticked away, the music started. I held the buzzer tightly.

"First You Say You Do."

"No!" shouted the host. Only a few seconds to go, and the music kept playing.

"Then You Say You Don't."

"No!"

In the wings, the producers had written the title of the song in big letters on a cue card for me to see and waved it in the air frantically, to get my attention. It was their money to give away, and I guess they wanted me to stay on the show. But I thought it would be cheating to look, so I didn't.

Years later, there was a lot of scandal about how TV game shows were rigged, and I guess this was one way it happened. Obviously, they knew which songs I knew and which ones my opponent didn't know. Because I was so wacky, they wanted to keep me on the show. I did win six hundred dollars and bought a new winter coat with some of my winnings. I was very proud of that coat, and I will never forget the title of the song I missed, "Undecided." Within a few months, I was asked to go back on the program. They wanted me to wear a brown wig and play the cousin of the girl who had been on a few months before—me. That show was a stepping stone that led to my first agent, Ray Powers, at Ashley Famous Artists.

I continued my studies at the American Academy of Dramatic Arts. The teachers decided I shouldn't take voice lessons, that my voice was unique, with a Jean Arthur quality. However, my agent thought my voice sounded like chickens scratching, and he sent me to a voice coach.

The coach lived in an old brownstone with a dark interior. When I met her, she made a scary impression. Her hair looked like a mass of gray cotton candy blown by the wind into an uncontrollable frenzy.

She asked me to try to lift her heavy oak desk as I repeated, "fee fi fo fum," each time putting the emphasis on "fee" or "fo" or "fum" while lowering my voice deeper and deeper with each word.

When I stepped out of the dark into the bright lights of New York City, I had a backache and I sounded like Tallulah Bankhead. But as I continued to speak, I sounded like an adolescent boy, going from low to high tones in the middle of a sentence. My parents decided this was not a wise use of funds, so no more voice lessons.

*

At the end of Jimmy's sophomore year at Harvard, he was asked to star in a Disney film, "Third Man on the Mountain," to be shot in Switzerland. Pretty good summer job. Jim's Mom asked me if I would like to travel to Europe with her to visit him. Of course I was thrilled! But my mother felt it wasn't proper to make such a trip unless Jim and I were engaged. (Or was she pushing for the union of her only daughter into this famous theatrical family?) Jimmy really wanted me to visit him in Switzerland. So on Mother's Day, 1958, he knocked on the door to his mother's bedroom and presented me as her Mother's Day gift—we were engaged. I don't know how thrilled she was, but she acted appropriately with tears, laughter, and hugs of congratulation. (Don't forget, she was a very good actress.) We weren't going to marry for at least three years—Jimmy had to finish at Harvard, and I wanted to complete my studies at the Academy.

A few days later in Nyack, the door to my guest room opened. It was Helen, carrying a breakfast tray. She entered, put the tray on my lap, and sat down on the edge of the bed next to me. Putting her hand on mine, she said, "Joyce, my darling, I don't think you should marry Jim. He isn't good enough for you."

I was shocked! Why was she saying this?

"I love Jimmy. I love him so much! I know he has done some bad things but he's still young, and as long as he knows I love him and you love him, he'll be OK."

I was biting my lip and trying not to cry. I was so confused and hurt for Jimmy. How could a mother say this about her child? Was it because he was adopted? Jim loved his father, and I think he wanted to emulate him in every way. Charlie MacArthur was witty, charming, loved the ladies, and drank to excess. Eventually he died of alcoholism. Jim was always fun to be with after his first two drinks. Then, all of a sudden, he would have one more sip and turn into a mean, frightening person. He was very clever about separating the people with whom he drank heavily and those he didn't. When necessary, he could hide that dark, shadowy side of himself.

Is this why Helen said what she did that morning in the guest room? Had she seen Jim after too much alcohol? Had his behavior reminded her of her beloved Charlie, who had hurt her many times? Was she trying to protect me? I remembered she had once threatened to send him back to his mother in Los Angeles.

"Please," I begged, "Don't ever tell him about his birth mother. It would break his heart. He thinks of you as his mother and he loves you so much." I thought that's why he did such mean things—he felt unloved. I just knew that if the two of us loved him enough, he would be just fine.

She patted my hand and said, "I love you very much." Slowly she rose from the bed. At the door, she turned and said, "If

Looking over our scene

you ever have any problems with Jim, you must never come to me." She closed the door behind her.

I sat looking at my breakfast, unable to take a single bite. I was dumbfounded and confused. At that moment I knew I must marry Jimmy; then he'd know that someone really loved him. How could a mother say such a thing? No wonder he drank and said mean things sometimes. He was a very hurt soul. My young ego said, "I can fix that!"

Helen planned the most incredible trip to Europe for her future daughter-in-law. First stop was Munich, Germany, and then we motored through the beautiful Tegernsee Valley to Rothenburg. We met Footie in Stuttgart, where Helen purchased a new Mercedes. Footie drove us through the rugged mountains to the quaint village of Zermatt, where Jimmy was filming. We gazed in wonder at the magnificent splendor of the Matterhorn, rising out of the green valley to touch the clear blue sky. At night, when the sky was sapphire blue and the moon shone on the snow-covered peak, it looked like the diamond glistening in my engagement ring.

We all dined together that evening in a charming little Swiss restaurant, where we stuffed ourselves with cheese fondue. I was so happy to see Jimmy. During the day I would walk up the mountainside with him to the location where he was filming. We'd pass herds of cows, their bells ringing just as my heart was. For fun, Helen and I did a small walk-on in the film. (Don't blink or you'll miss us.)

As the time grew near to leave, Jimmy and I climbed up the side of the mountain and sat looking down over the village below. I looked like a young Swiss girl in a dirndl dress, with my long blonde hair piled on top of my head. Would there ever be a time when we would feel so in love again? When we became engaged, it had been with the idea of waiting a few years to be married. During filming, Jim decided he didn't want to go back to Harvard. He wanted to pursue his acting career. Jimmy was tanned, his sandy blond hair more golden from the Swiss sun. He looked at me through those blue eyes.

"Would you mind not waiting to marry me? Let's get married as soon as I get home."

I was unprepared but thrilled. "You mean in two months, when you come home?"

"Yes. OK?" Sitting in a field of wildflowers, surrounded by snow-covered mountains, I smiled and said, "Oh, Jimmy, I can't wait to be your wife."

THREE

Little Girl Lost

From my bedroom window I could see the moon shining on the Matterhorn. I couldn't believe I would be Mrs. James MacArthur. It seemed like a fairytale. As I drifted off to sleep, I thought back to my childhood.

"Daddy, Daddy! I called for my handsome, sweet Daddy. Down the hall I heard my mother's voice.

"Joyce, honey, come here."

Balancing the little tea set Daddy had given me for my sixth birthday, I couldn't wait to surprise him with make-believe tea and white-bread squares for tea sandwiches.

Mother was sitting in bed. She patted the empty space next to her.

"Come up here, sweetheart, next to me."

Little me

I climbed up and snuggled into her arms. She smelled sweet. Her curly brown hair, which had been blonde like mine when she was little, fell around her face and framed her green eyes. Tucked next to her, I felt her softness and warmth.

"Where's Daddy?"

A moment's pause. "Honey, your Daddy's gone... I asked him to leave. He's not coming back."

Always the obedient child, I didn't ask why.

I shrank into myself and pressed hard against the pillow. I couldn't breathe, couldn't cry. I just stared into space, that empty space where there was no Daddy.

*

For a short time Mother and I lived in Baltimore with my grandparents. It was a secure and happy time for me, but I missed Daddy. My grandparents lived in an old house that had been converted into three small apartments. The closets smelled like mothballs, but the kitchen where Grandmother Muz cooked smelled delicious. On Christmas Eve, now that I was seven, I was allowed to stay up late and decorate the small tree in the living room with my grandmother. I threw long strings of silvery icicles on the branches. In the morning I awoke to see

My Daddy

what was under the tree. The two gifts I most wanted were a sewing box and a high chair for my doll, but no gift in the whole wide world could have been greater: my Daddy! I rushed to him and sat for the longest time folded in his arms like a small package. The sewing box and high chair were hardly noticed.

Later the next day, I walked between Mommy and Daddy down the streets of Baltimore, past the freshly-washed marble steps leading to the row houses, each decorated with beautiful Christmas lights or blue Hanukkah lights in celebration of this wondrous time of year. But my own private celebration was that Mommy and Daddy told me they were going to get married again! They swung me up in the air as we got closer and closer to the big stone courthouse where we would become a family again. I sat on a hard wooden chair, my legs sticking straight out. I looked past my shiny patent leather Mary Jane shoes to Mommy and Daddy standing in line in front of a window. Suddenly, I saw Mother start to cry, then rush toward me, grab my hand and abruptly drag me out of the building into the clouded winter sky. I tried to keep up as she walked swiftly down the street. She was pulling me along, tears streaming down her face. Through her sobs, Mother tried to tell me she couldn't go through with marrying Daddy again. A chill ran through my body until it numbed me all over.

After Christmas, I was sent to a nearby Episcopal girls' orphanage. Mother must have been a very proud woman; she didn't want to overstay or take advantage of living with my grandmother. I didn't know where Daddy went, but once again, he was gone.

The orphanage was in an old, foreboding mansion. The expansive grounds were loaded with huge pine trees whose heavy boughs swept the lawn. The room I slept in had four beds on either side of the room. At the foot of the bed was a footlocker, and a laundry bag was tied to the end of each bed. The first night I was there, I had to use the bathroom and crept out of bed in the dark, feeling my way along the row of beds toward the light in the hallway. But just as I reached the doorway, I wet myself. I was so ashamed. I took off my nightgown and used it to wipe away all evidence, then felt my way back to my bed and stuffed the dirty nighty into my laundry bag. I put on a clean one and climbed into bed. I buried my head in my pillow so no one would hear me cry. In the morning a lady named Miss Hope (funny, her name was everything I had lost) braided my hair. With each twist she yanked so hard it made tears stand in my eyes. I kept remembering what Mother had said when she left me there, "You must be a good little girl."

Every night when I went to sleep I prayed for my Daddy. I didn't know where he was, and I missed him so much. Mother would come visit me on Sundays. There were other children who were not as fortunate as I; their mothers didn't come, and I felt sad for them.

Sometime that same year (I was still in second grade), Mother and I moved to Jacksonville, Florida. I was now to stay with a lady in the country who took in small children. The place looked like the house of the old lady in the shoe, with children everywhere, inside and out. A bed sheet, wet with urine, was hung out to shame a small boy who had wet his bed. I held my mother's hand and stayed close by her side. With all my heart I did not want to stay there, but I said nothing. I know my mother wished there was some other way, but she must have had no other choice.

I slept in a tiny room with three other girls. In the morning we all crowded into a small dining room and sat on benches, eating oatmeal that was surely meant for library paste. No one would help me braid my hair, which was long and very fine. My young fingers couldn't manage the braids, and as we walked along the dirt road to school, my ribbons fell out of my hair. My hair a shambles, I arrived at school ashamed that I was made to wear the same dress all week long.

We were known as "the children from the home."

One Saturday, Mother came to take me into town. At the end of our day together we sat side by side on the bus as we rode back to the country. I sat very quietly next to my mother, afraid that if I spoke I would burst into tears. I dug my fingernails into the palms of my hands, trying to make one pain, the one I could control, take the place of another. When we reached our destination, Mother helped me down the steps of the bus. The door made a swishing sound as it closed behind us. We walked down the street toward the house filled with children, but without joy. Just steps from the front door, I couldn't control my emotions any longer. I started to sob so hard that my body shook. I hung my head—I couldn't look at Mother, since I wasn't her "good little girl." I knew I wasn't being brave. After a moment I gathered enough courage and through my sobs, begged her not to leave me. Mother understood; she said I didn't have to stay there. I was so relieved I ran into the house and up to my room to pack my suitcase. Downstairs, Mother talked to the lady who owned the house.

Knees trembling, I sheepishly carried my belongings down the stairs. As I hit the bottom step, Mother rounded the corner with the lady at her heels, screaming, "Who wants her? She's a goddamned spoiled rotten brat!"

I was certain it was true.

Our next home was near the beach in Jacksonville. Mother and I lived in a garage that had been converted into a bedroom and bath. We had to wear shower caps to bed at night to keep the flying cockroaches out of our hair. In the morning before Mother went to work, she would give me change to buy breakfast at the coffee shop. I was in second grade. I liked my teacher very much, but I had such a hard time learning that I really didn't like to go. So I often took my breakfast change and lunch money and made a beeline for the boardwalk at the beach. There it was such fun! I would have a breakfast of cotton candy or sometimes a bright red candied apple. Then with my lunch money I would ride the Ferris wheel. Often after I depleted my funds, I had no qualms about asking complete strangers for extra change for more rides.

It was soon after these escapades that I was to stay in another home. A lady took in children at the beach, near where Mother had secured a job as the social director in a hotel. There weren't as many children in this home. At the age of eight, I was allowed to babysit some of the younger ones, a responsibility that made me feel very grown up. For hours on end I would entertain the littlest children. Sometimes I would enlist the help of older children in the neighborhood to help me string an old Army blanket across the doorway between the living room and the dining room—a makeshift curtain for my miniature stage. I'd line up flashlights on the floor facing the curtain—my footlights. The idea of doing plays must have stemmed from the thrill I had portraying the red cow in a Christmas play at the orphanage. I remember my line, "I was the cow all white and red who gave Jesus straw for his bed."

Now I had graduated to a much larger role. I was Cinderella! I gave my playmates minor roles. Well, I was the writer, producer, and director! One day I was especially excited; we were to give a performance after supper and invite all the neighborhood children. We spent hours making tickets out of construction paper. A lot of children and their parents said they would come. We spent all day cleaning the house, counting our tickets, and testing our curtain to make sure it would slide on the rope. Early in the day I had carefully wrapped each strand of my hair around a sock and knotted the toe and top together to make curls.

Before supper and our evening performance I took the children to the beach to play. I must have been quite a sight, an eight-year-old with a head full of colorful socks tied to my hair, parading down the street followed by my even younger charges.

As we were making sand castles, the sun was on its journey to the sea, making magnificent colors of pink, purples, oranges and reds in the clouds.

"Look, you can see the shape of a dog! Oh, no! It looks more like a cat. Can you see it?" I loved to make objects out of the colored clouds. As I turned back from the edge of the sea, my bucket filled with water, I noticed a man approaching far down the beach. I put my hand over my eyes against the setting sun and there, walking in the golden sunlight and carrying a little box, was my Daddy. I dropped my bucket and ran as fast as I could toward him, colored socks flopping against my head.

"Oh, Daddy, Daddy!" He picked me up and hugged me tight. It was the best hug ever! He gently set me down and kneeled in the sand.

"Well, I'll be a humdinger, if you don't look something wonderful, socks and all, sweetie. I'm so happy to see you, Darlin.'" He handed me the beautifully wrapped box he had been carrying.

His Virginia accent was music to me. He was very handsome, with soft blue eyes. My tears flowed down my cheeks just as water flowed from my hastily dropped bucket. I was so happy—my Prince had found me! Sitting in the sand, I peeled away the paper and unwrapped the gift. I carefully took out a little blue music box with a porcelain picture on the top. The picture was a man in old-fashioned attire on bended knee, holding the hand of a beautiful young maiden under a willow tree. When I lifted the top, the tinkling music box played "Let Me Call You Sweetheart."

Hand in hand, Daddy and I walked back to the house with my young charges following. After supper that night, my hair was relieved of colored socks. In their place, long blonde ringlets. The flashlights were lined up and turned on, the blanket was pulled aside and I made my entrance as Cinderella. Sitting on the floor, legs crossed, and several heads taller than the neighborhood children was my Daddy. I can't think of another performance when I felt so happy.

Shortly after seeing Daddy, Mother said we were moving again. I don't know where my Daddy went, but he was gone again. This time I was to live in an apartment on Oak Street in the city of Jacksonville. How wonderful, I was going to live with Mother! I went to a red brick school several blocks from our little apartment. My new teacher's name was Mrs. Kraut. She was very stern, heavy-set, and not the least bit friendly. My favorite classes were art and recess. Reading, writing and arithmetic remained a mystery to me, but I sat quietly in the back of the room, trying to go unnoticed.

Mother was working and didn't come home until hours after I had finished school. On my way home from school, I often stopped in a church and sat quietly, taking in the beauty of the stained glass windows. Sometimes I would kneel and say a child's made-up prayer, as the soft organ music drifted through the eaves of the church. Here I felt safe and loved.

Going to Sunday school was my reward for getting through a grueling week of school. I would raise my voice loudly to the strains of "Jesus Loves Me." My faith was never forced on me; it came from deep inside my soul. This faith protected me and gave me strength as a child and continues to give me strength as an adult. My mother reinforced my deepest feelings about a God—a Divine Spirit—that watches over each of us. Great faith has helped me through many difficult times.

One Sunday, walking to church with two nickels in my hand, one for the offering and one for a donut after Sunday school, I carelessly dropped a nickel down the drain in the gutter. I raised my eyes to heaven and said, "Sorry, God, that was your nickel."

On school days I would come home and throw myself across the bed I shared with Mother and listen hour after hour to radio shows: "Stella Dallas, Backstage Wife," "Pepper Young's Family," and my very favorite, "Sky King, brought to you by Skippy Peanut Butter." Boy, did I ever want a decoder ring! In order to get one, I had to write a letter telling why I liked Skippy Peanut Butter. I tried and tried but couldn't spell the words I wanted to say. Finally I asked a friend to write the letter for me, saying that I liked Skippy Peanut Butter because it didn't stick to the roof of my mouth. The day the ring arrived, I was thrilled.

My early days in show business continued with shows I staged in the garage of our apartment building. For one show I borrowed a little white picket fence that bordered a neighbor's flowerbed and a straw cowboy hat from one of the young boys in our building. For one cent you could me see stand in the center of the picket fence wearing a cowboy hat and singing, "Don't Fence Me In." I was a hit!

After I finished third grade (heaven knows how! I didn't know any more than when I started first grade), we packed up and moved to St. Petersburg, Florida. We lived in a tiny cinder block house landscaped with crushed seashells and sharp Bermuda grass. One day I walked to the beach and into a little general store to buy candy. As I waited for my change, with a red jawbreaker in my mouth—getting it wet enough to rub on my lips so it would look like lipstick—I noticed a picture on the bulletin board of a young girl with braids who looked a lot like me. Removing the jawbreaker and still tasting the hot cinnamon flavor, I stepped behind the counter to get a closer look. It was me!

"Excuse me, Sir!"

He gave me a stern look. I realized I shouldn't be behind the counter. I returned to the customer side. "Would you please read what it says under that picture, because that's me."

The man looked closely at the picture and back to me. I put the jawbreaker back in my mouth and tried to smile like the young girl in the picture. He looked at me quizzically, and I nervously spit the sticky jawbreaker into my hand and smiled again.

"Well, I'll be—it sure is you, little girl. It says…" He put his glasses on and read very slowly. It seemed a lifetime to me. "It says, 'Please help me find my daughter.'" Looking closer, he said, "And there's a telephone number."

"Could you please call my Daddy for me, Sir?" I felt so excited but full of questions. Why didn't Daddy know where I was? Was he all right?

Thank heavens, the candy seller reached Daddy, who told me to stay where I was. When he came through the door, I rushed into his arms, so happy to see him. We hugged and he cried.

"Your Mommy didn't want me to know where you were. She has her reasons, I guess, but I just wanted to know you were all right."

I don't know what transpired between my mother and father, but within a few days I was allowed to go sailing with Daddy in a rented sailboat on the bay. Drifting along through the water, I again felt secure with Daddy at the helm. However, the smooth sailing wasn't to last. Mother, with only a quarter in her pocket, took a job as the junior social director at the quite swell Vinoy Park Hotel, a grand old pink building in St. Petersburg. She was required to live at the hotel but wasn't allowed to have me with her. Again she had to find a place for me to stay. We went to Tampa, Florida, a city near St. Petersburg. Hand in hand, we stood outside the archway of an old Spanish building. Looking down the veranda, I saw a black figure gliding toward us, as if on skates. Squinting, I tried to make out the mysterious form as it glided closer and closer. It looked like an angel dressed in black. Her hands were folded inside her full black sleeves, and she had a white band around her head with a flowing black veil. Mother leaned down and whispered, "If you're very good, they may let you live here." I remembered seeing nuns when I accompanied one of my Catholic friends to her church. I thought it was a wonderful thing to be able to marry Jesus and help people. What a heavenly thought! If I lived here, maybe I could help people and marry Jesus, too. It was so quiet and peaceful; I knew I would feel good here.

My mother and the nun exchanged a few words. I only heard part of what was being said. "I'm very sorry, my dear. If your little girl isn't Catholic, she may not stay here." My mother looked down at me. All hope had left her hazel eyes.

The angel lady in black continued, "However, there is a lady who takes in children; her home is right behind us."

Mother smiled in my direction, "Could you please tell me her name?"

"It's Mrs. Rose. She may have room for your little girl." She smiled gently, apologetically, and placed her hand on my head. "God bless you, child."

She turned and glided back, the light catching her form as she drifted in and out of the shadows of the sunlit archways covered with beautiful hanging flowers. My angel was gone, and again I felt very little and very lost.

Mrs. Rose's house was impressive. Maybe this wouldn't be so bad after all. She seemed quite nice. After showing us her home, which extended around a courtyard, she opened the door to a room with three small beds and a baby crib. A two-year-old baby boy was fast asleep in the crib.

"This will be your room, Joyce." It was a pretty room, with its very own adjoining bathroom. She explained that the children shared the bathroom. I was happy to see the baby boy and thought that I could help take care of him. When I was six, I had a make-believe child that was always with me. Now maybe Mrs. Rose would let me help her with a real baby. I smiled at my mother and pressed her hand, trying to reassure her that I would be fine here.

At first it was very nice. I was going to a new school and liked my teacher very much. She read to us. I'll never forget the Nancy Drew mystery she read every day after lunch. I couldn't wait! How wonderful to be able to read! I was now in fourth grade and still didn't have a clue how to read. It would have been wonderful to be able to escape into the world of books, with new friends and stories with happy endings.

Mrs. Rose's house was very nice, but she wasn't. She was mean and impatient with the baby. One night when I was in the bathroom brushing my teeth before bed, Mrs. Rose picked him up and stood him on top of the toilet seat. Then she took a washcloth with scalding water and pressed it to his face. He started screaming. His face turned bright red where she had placed the cloth. When she reached to put more hot water on the cloth, I grabbed the steaming cloth out of her hand and started hitting her with it as hard as I could. She reached for me, but I ran away. I was very frightened and terribly angry with Mrs. Rose. I called my father. I don't remember whose phone I used or how, but I do remember he came that very night from Sarasota to get me. I was afraid to tell my mother because I would once again have disappointed her. Couldn't I ever be a brave little girl?

Daddy took me to his rundown fishing boat in Sarasota. After Mother and Father divorced, he became a charter fisherman and lived on his boat. That night I lay in a wooden bunk and looked around the small rugged cabin of the Bonita. The smell of salt water and fish filled the air, soft waves lapped against the hull and rocked me gently side to side. I fell asleep with the sound of the water and the creaking of the boat, which filled my ears with a special kind of music.

In the morning I turned to see Daddy sleeping soundly in the bunk across from me. He was a mighty handsome sea captain. I climbed out of my bunk and rummaged through the cabinets in the galley. I found a can of baked beans and made a baked bean and ketchup sandwich on Wonder Bread. There were lemons and sugar, for lemonade. What a great breakfast for my Daddy! He ate every morsel and looked at me as if I was the best little girl in the world. But what would my mother think?

Daddy found a lady with the storybook name of Mrs. Lillycrop for me to stay with. She was the local school dietician and the widow of an Episcopalian minister. Mrs. Lillycrop took care of one other child, Bobby. For dinner, she made delicious goodies for us, like fresh tomatoes and cucumbers soaked in vinegar and sugar. She was a pretty lady who looked like a perfect grandmother. Her home was a tidy yellow house with green striped awnings to shade the hot Florida sun.

When Mrs. Lillycrop's daughter was to be married, she made a beautiful tulle dress with a pattern of little roses for me to wear. I felt very special. I wore the dress again on Easter Sunday, and a straw hat with pink ribbons that hung down my back. Daddy gave me a corsage of little pink roses. I felt happy kneeling in church, listening to the minister pray. But suddenly the heat, the fragrance of all the beautiful Easter lilies (and maybe too many marshmallow chickens from my Easter basket) caused my head to spin and my knees to buckle. I passed out right there in church in the middle of the Ten Commandments.

When I came to, I was lying in the back seat of someone's car. Mrs. Lillycrop was waving a fan with Jesus' picture on it in front of my face. For a moment, I thought I had passed through the pearly gates and Jesus himself was swaying above my head. By evening, I had recovered from my embarrassing state and dug into a dinner of baked ham, potato salad, cornbread, and sweet iced tea.

All the time I was living with Mrs. Lillycrop and visiting Daddy on his fishing boat, Mother continued to work at the Vinoy Park Hotel in St. Petersburg. I didn't hear from Mother very often. I imagined that she was working hard, but someplace down deep I was afraid she was angry with me because I had gone to be with Daddy.

Every evening after dinner, Daddy would come and take me for a walk. He'd carry a stick and when I wasn't looking he would tap the back of my leg and tell me there was a little man following us. I liked this game, but most of all I loved it when he would sing to me like Bing Crosby. Daddy would croon, "I'm gonna buy a paper doll that I can call my own," or "Peg of my heart, I love you."

Later I learned Daddy built kitchen cabinets for Mrs. Lillycrop as payment for my lodging. On the weekends, I stayed on the boat and made baked bean sandwiches and lemonade, not only for Daddy but also for all the fishermen on the dock. And I continued my early show business career. I'd set up my phonograph player on the bow of the boat. When the fishermen docked at the end of the day, they could find me dancing the hula and giving out little baked bean sandwiches left over from breakfast.

How I passed fourth grade, heaven only knows. I didn't know one multiplication table. School was over, and so was my stay on the Bonita and life with sweet Mrs. Lillycrop.

I took the bus down the Tamiami Trail to Clearwater, Florida, to live with my mother, who had a new job as manager of the beachfront Yacht Basin Apartments. She was in charge of two hundred apartments, with an apartment of her own. I would now have my very own bedroom, painted sunshine yellow. The window in my room looked out over Clearwater Bay, and Mother's room was across from mine. We had a nice living room with a dining area. I was very proud that Mother had such an important position and was given a limousine to drive. Well, it was long like a limousine—but it was a hearse. I was happy to live with my mother again. Of course I missed Daddy, but he was near enough for me to hop on the bus and head up the Tamiami Trail to visit him once in a while.

I was able to get through the fifth and sixth grades in much the same manner as I had passed the others. Not only did I do trash and erasers, but included in my repertoire of tricks was washing the blackboard, dropping my book or rushing to the girls' room when it was time to read. For extra insurance, I plucked a lovely flower from the flowerbed of our apartment house and laid it on the teacher's desk. I could have written a handbook, "How to Slide Through School by Being a Good Little Girl When You Can't Read or Spell."

One Christmas, Mother and I put up a pretty little Christmas tree in the living room. Mother cleverly mixed ivory soap flakes with water into a thick paste to put on the tree branches for snow. It looked beautiful. On Christmas day, Daddy arrived with a box of Whitman chocolates for me. When I opened the box, a five-dollar bill was taped to the top inside. I gave Daddy a big hug and thanked him. He looked at me sadly, "Honey, I had a car full of gifts for you but someone broke in and stole them. I'm so sorry." I hated to see my Daddy so sad.

I put my arms around him. "Daddy, I love you so much. It's my favorite candy and I can get something wonderful with the money." I could feel the tension between my mother and father. I felt sorry for Daddy, but the Whitman sampler and a hug from my Daddy were enough of a gift for me. After he left, Mother said, "His car wasn't broken into. He only said that. He doesn't really love you, or he would give us money." I hated her when she said bad things about my father, which she often did.

After school my friends and I would go running across the sugar-white Florida sand and jump screaming with joy into the blue-green water of the Gulf of Mexico. I would swim underwater and, in the silence, black out all unpleasantness in the world, including the difficulties that I had learning in school. I'd push myself off the sandy bottom to the surface, gasp for air and sink again into a blissfully silent world. Sometimes I would sit on the bottom of the ocean and think about what I would do after graduation from sixth grade. I could imagine myself as a majorette, marching down the football field, leading the band and tossing my baton high over my head.

Mother knocked on my bedroom door and delivered devastating news.

"We're moving to New York City."

New York City! She wanted me to leave the beaches I loved so much and the friends I had made, to move to a city with gangsters. What in the world was she thinking? "You're going to go to a lovely school in the city, Miss Hewitt's School for Girls."

A girls' school! She must be kidding! At twelve years old, I had just started to like boys. A girls' school, no way! Recently I'd lived in the same place two whole years and had made friends. Now she wanted me to leave all of this behind and move to a city of steel and glass and... gangsters!

I buried my head in my pillow and cried all night.

Mercifully, my mother's boyfriend, Charles, thought the bucolic setting of Solebury, a small boarding school in New Hope, Pennsylvania, would be a happier place for me to live and learn. At least Solebury was coed. The girls' campus was a mile away from the boys' but we had classes together.

FOUR

Back to the Fairy Tale

Times were often sad and confusing for me when I was a little girl, but now thoughts of my childhood faded away. I had a whole new wonderful life ahead. I said a prayer thanking God and made a vow never to get divorced. I would never hurt my children the way I had been hurt.

Leaving Jimmy in Europe was a little less difficult because in a few short months, we would be married. After our sad farewell, Footie drove Helen and me over the mountains into Italy for the last leg of our journey. We stopped at Lake Como, where she and I shared the most beautiful room overlooking the lake.

While we were dressing in the huge marble bathroom, Helen started talking about disinheriting Jimmy. I didn't know where the thought had come from, or why she was expressing it at that very moment. These sudden outbursts about Jimmy puzzled me. Of course, I said nothing.

Looking back, I wonder if she thought if she disinherited Jimmy, I wouldn't marry him. Was she trying to find out if I was only interested in family money, or was she trying to find a way to save me? Or was she really thinking of disinheriting him? It was such a strange thing to say at that moment.

The next day we motored on to Rome, where we shared a room at the Excelsior Hotel. We were too excited to sleep because the next morning, we were to have an audience with Pope Pius XII! Helen was a devout Catholic.

We were both in bed trying to sleep when suddenly, she threw off the covers and sprang out of bed. She suggested that we practice genuflecting and kissing the Pope's ring. All night we were up and down on our knees, in our nighties, kissing each other's rings and giggling. I'm certain the laughter came from nervousness about the importance of the meeting.

In the morning, exhausted from lack of sleep, we dressed like young novices in long black dresses and black lace mantillas on our heads. Footie met us in the hotel lobby. The three of us sat in the back seat of a car the Vatican had sent. Excited and nervous, we spoke not a word as we made our journey through the streets of Rome.

St. Peter's Basilica was breathtaking. Once inside, we were led by Swiss guards past throngs of people who were squeezed behind red velvet ropes. We followed the guards to a special area beside the Great Altar. The three of us walked side by side, squeezing each other's hands. Footie was Catholic too. Even though I was a lowly Methodist, at this moment I felt as if I were about to enter heaven's gates.

Eight carved wooden chairs with red velvet seats stood in a neat row beside the altar. Three of the chairs were reserved for us. After we were seated, the colorfully dressed Swiss guards stood by us. Surely I was dreaming.

Shouts of "Papa! Papa!" echoed through the vast recesses of the cathedral, then loud applause. Seated on a red velvet sedan chair, the Pope appeared, carried high above the frenzied crowds. I felt as if I would faint in the midst of such emotion. The Pope, all in white with a small ermine cape draped over his narrow shoulders, leaned over the crowd and made the sign of the cross. As he came close to us it seemed as if he looked me right in the eyes and made the sign of the cross. I froze. Helen took my arm and Footie the other. She said, "Imagine that—he looked right at you!" I was speechless.

After the Pope's platform was lowered near the main altar, he rose from his throne and crossed the marble floor to the Altar of St. Peter. As he walked up the steps to the first level of the altar, he took a slight skip, revealing his red velvet slippers. Then he sat on an even grander throne at the foot of the altar. He was so small. Welcoming each visitor from afar, he spoke many different languages. At the end of his bene-diction, he stepped down to bless the Cardinals who were seated below the throne. A Swiss guard beckoned us to come over to the throne for our audience with the Pope.

Knees shaking and moving as if by remote control, we approached. I was completely in awe of the sights, sounds, and religious significance of the moment.

The Pope had his back to us, his small white figure surrounded by the vibrant red colors worn by the Cardinals. Suddenly, he turned and headed straight across the marble floor, in front of the Great Altar surrounded by columns, and walked in a direct line… right to me.

The Pope reached out his hand, and in a flash, as if struck by light-ning, I fell to my knees and kissed the ring on his outstretched hand. He looked into my eyes and smiled, then turned and walked away. I wondered if he was confused and thought I was the First Lady of the American Theater! Whatever he thought, it was a moment I shall never forget. Jim's mother was thrilled for me; she said the Pope may have had an eye for a young girl who looked so innocent and devout.

The next day Footie drove us further down the boot of Italy. We took a boat to the isle of Capri and visited Gracie Field's home and the hotel she owned by the sea. At lunch I sat among the very famous, with Gracie Fields on one side and the very funny Bea Lillie on the other. Also joining the festivities was Lucky Luciano. I didn't know at the time that he was a famous gangster.

I was on my best behavior, but Bea Lillie wasn't. She whispered naughty ditties in my ear, while I tried not to laugh. She sang, "Little Old Lady Passing By," but instead she sang in my ear, "Little Old Lady Passing Wind." Suddenly she grabbed my hand and said, "I'm taking Joyce shopping!' She pulled me up the stairs to hail a horse-drawn carriage. We climbed into the back and clop-clopped to the Village Square. She guided me to a little dress shop, and, to my astonishment, she stripped me to my undies and proceeded to dress me head-to-toe in new clothes.

"These clothes are much more appropriate and chic for the likes of you!" She had outfitted me in brightly colored Capri pants, a beautiful emerald green jacket, and a little skull cap on my head, just like her signature cap. She insisted on paying for the outfit. Then, stepping into the warm Capri sunshine, she bought two lemon ices from a street vendor. We were buddies. I was so lucky to have these wonderful ladies treat me so kindly!

A few days later, Helen and I said farewell to Footie and boarded our ship, the Giulio Cesare, to sail back to New York. A telegram from Jimmy was waiting on board for us: "Bon voyage to the two ladies I love the most."

When we docked in New York City, the press was waiting. They took pictures of us, and the next day the headlines of the New York papers announced, "Getting to Know Her" and "Helen Hayes's Son, James MacArthur, to Marry."

Before we disembarked, I felt a deep sadness as we said good-bye to each other. It wasn't just "I'm going to miss you for a while," but something stronger. We had been so close, had shared so much, and now I was going to be her daughter-in-law. Would that change everything? Why this empty, lost feeling as we parted? I felt it and thought she did too. Was she thinking of what she had said to me in the guest room that morning, about not marrying Jimmy?

Getting to Know Her. Helen Hayes arriv from Europe aboa Giulio Cesare at Pier 84. With her is son's fiancee, Joyce Bulifant.

While waiting for Jim to return from Switzerland and finishing up my classes at the Academy, I worked as a background dancer on the television show, "Arthur Murray's Dance Party," filmed live at the old Ziegfeld Theater in New York. In a pale blue tulle dress supplied by the show, I waltzed around the stage in the background with the other dancers. All the dancing ladies wore similar pastel dresses.

When Helen watched the show on TV, she had a hard time picking me out from all the other dancers, so she bought me a white dotted Swiss formal with puffy sleeves and large brightly-colored flowers in the fabric. The first time I wore my new colorful formal, Helen, watching television in Nyack, was able to single me out very easily. The problem was that all eyes were on the young blonde girl floating through the waltz in her brightly-colored dress, not on Catherine and Arthur Murray, the stars of the show. The following week I was asked, none too graciously, to wear the faded blue dress again, and to tone down my dancing.

Planning our wedding filled the rest of the summer. We decided to be married in the chapel close to Solebury, our school. We decided on a small, unpretentious wedding with a reception at Mother and Dad's home afterwards.

Lily Lodge, the daughter of Francesca and Ambassador John Lodge, was my maid of honor. She had become a good friend and was very close to the MacArthur family; as a young actress, she had lived in Nyack with them.

Jim wanted Footie as his best man, but because he was Catholic and we were being married in an Episcopal church, Footie's bishop wouldn't allow him to stand up for Jim. The bishop thought the marriage would get too much publicity and it wouldn't do to have a Catholic as best man in an Episcopal church. So our good friend, John Maxton-Graham, did the honors.

On November 2, 1958, our wedding day, it rained like the Great Floods. The tiny chapel was filled with wedding guests, and the brass chandeliers and the lighted candles gave a warm glow to the occasion. I teasingly told Jimmy that I would be very nervous.

"You'd better smile at me when Dad walks me down the aisle, or I'll pick up my skirts and run away!"

The music started. My arm was looped through Dad's, and I carried a beautiful bouquet. With each step down the aisle, my satin slippers peeked out from under my simple white satin gown.

Carefully placing one foot in front of the other in time to "The Wedding March," I looked up and saw Jim at the altar. Suddenly a giant smile crossed his face. From the front of the pew, the theatrically commanding voice of the First Lady of American Theater shouted, "Play it straight, Jim, play it straight!"

After the ceremony Helen apologized to the minister for her outburst. He said, with a reassuring smile, "I thought it was very motherly of you to tell your son to stand up straight."

The next day, our picture appeared on the front page of newspapers across the country with the caption "Helen Hayes's Son Marries."

We spent our first night as husband and wife at the Buccaneer Hotel on the island of St. Croix, in a pink bungalow overlooking the sea. We were both twenty years old. I wore a beautiful nightgown, which my mother had helped me choose, for my first night of love as

Mrs. James MacArthur. But later I sat huddled in a chair, arms around my knees and tears running down my cheeks. Across the room, my husband had passed out face down on our honeymoon bed.

It was the beginning of a pattern: Drink, act mean, apologize, act nice, drink. Every day I hoped there would be a new pattern, one that would begin a happy life together.

We did end up having a happy honeymoon, swimming, sailing, and drinking Planters Punch. There was lots of lovemaking, and I tried to forget the wedding night.

Wedding reception with Lily Lodge, Jim, Helen and Mother

FIVE

Not Happily Ever After

W
e rented an apartment on 80 East End Ave in New York City. They told us it had a view of the river. It did, if you stood on your tippy toes, twisted your neck like a contortionist, and looked out the corner of the bedroom window. We bought a new bed and inherited some furniture from Jim's parents. With money that Lilian Gish had given us as a wedding gift, I bought a bookcase, which we used as a room divider, making an area for a dining table and four chairs separate from the living room.

The flowers Dad sent once a week cheered up our apartment. The kitchen was a typically tiny New York kitchen—no window and no space. It was home, however, our first home, and I was going to be the best wife ever.

Our first morning, I awoke early to prepare breakfast for my husband. I mixed up batter for waffles so we could use our new waffle iron. I squeezed fresh orange juice, cut a cantaloupe in half and made little designs on the edges. I filled each half with fresh fruit. A small bouquet of flowers, new placemats and napkins made the table look elegant. Stepping back, I looked at the table with an approving smile.

I tiptoed into our bedroom and gently kissed Jimmy. "Breakfast is ready." When he came to the table, he picked up the orange juice, made a face and demanded angrily, "Where's the juice I want?"

"What juice would you like?"

"You know what I want! Where is it?"

Feeling anxious, I went to our kitchen and opened the cupboard.

"We have grape juice and pear nectar. Would you like that?"

I didn't understand why he was so angry.

Rising from the table, he came into the kitchen and put his face so close to mine that I backed away. Then he pushed me into the corner and yelled.

"What's wrong with you? Where is it? Where is it?"

I slid down in the corner, covered my face and tried not to cry. He stood over me and leaned into my face.

"You are so stupid, you're crazy!"

He turned and left me huddled on the kitchen floor. I got up and went into the bathroom and let the tears flow. Later I learned he wanted tomato juice. Believe me, I always kept tomato juice in the house after that.

Jim and I continued with our acting careers. One day Jimmy came home to tell me exciting news—they wanted him for a television show that would be filmed for two weeks in Hollywood. I was delighted.

"Oh Jimmy, that's so exciting! When do we go?"

He looked at me with disdain. "You're not going!"

"Oh."

Whenever Jimmy went to Hollywood, he chose to go alone. Of course I felt sad. I had long had an overwhelming need to be accepted.

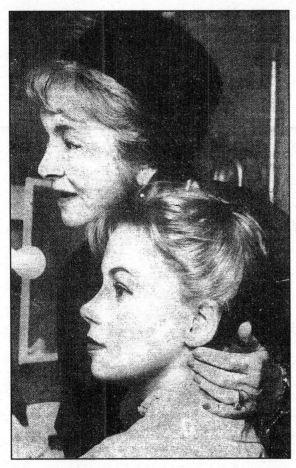

Opening night with Helen

My mother wanted me to be a good little girl, and now I wanted to be a good little wife. The fact that I was working helped me feel better about myself. It was during that time I acted in several television shows in New York: "Too Young to Go Steady," with Don Ameche and Tuesday Weld, produced by David Susskind, "Thérèse Raquin" with Eva La Gallienne for "Play of the Week," and "Naked City."

Jim and I auditioned for plays and we were each lucky to get roles on Broadway. Jim starred in Arthur Laurents' play, "Invitation to a March," with Celeste Holm and a beautiful young actress, Jane Fonda. I was in Lindsay and Crouse's play, "Tall Story," understudying the lead and playing a small role. Another up-and-coming young actor, Robert Redford, was also in the play.

On our days off, Jim and I spent wonderful weekends, alternating between learning to play bridge with Mother and Dad at the farm, and playing Scrabble and other word games with Helen in Nyack. Because

I couldn't spell, the word games always made me feel self-conscious and stupid. I dreaded seeing those board games come out. Often I would get a terrible stomach ache and retreat to the safety of the guest room. (At that time I didn't know that I was dyslexic. I just thought I was dumb.)

Once after the theater, Helen took me to Lindy's, famous for their cheesecake, where we met some of her friends. After introductions, one of them said, "You always have a smile on your face, Joyce."

Helen chirped, "Yes, she is just a grinning idiot." I smiled outwardly and cried inwardly. Maybe she was making a joke, but my insecurity at the time made me believe she was right. In many ways I felt I was an idiot.

Dinner in Nyack was always wonderful. The most creative people shared stories around the dining table. Jimmy's Uncle Alfred, playwright Ben Hecht—with whom Mr. MacArthur had written "The Front Page" and "Twentieth Century"—the great stage actress Katherine Cornell, and silent screen star, Lillian Gish. Lillian was Jim's godmother. I called her my "fairy godmother" because she was good to me in so many ways. What a fortunate young girl I was to be in such company!

✳

Jim was offered another Disney movie, to be filmed in Scotland— "Kidnapped," starring Peter Finch. We traveled to Europe on the Sylvania, a small ship of the Cunard Line. When we reached our stateroom, we found it loaded with baskets of fruit and bouquets of flowers. Sitting in a green velvet chair and running my hand over the satin bedspread, I felt like a princess. Every afternoon, just like a proper English

Sailing to England

couple, we had tea.

Upon arriving in London, we stayed at the elegant Dorchester Hotel, compliments of Walt Disney, who always treated his actors to the best. In our magnificent suite, we had a sitting room with a fireplace and a grand piano, on which sat a huge vase of beautiful spring flowers. Double doors opened to our bedroom and a spacious marble bathroom with big fluffy white towels on heated racks.

In the morning, Jimmy was driven to Pinewood Studios for wardrobe fittings and I was left to explore London. I stopped by the florist inside the hotel and bought some lily-of-the-valley to pin on my new black suit. Wearing black patent leather heels, white pearls, proper cotton gloves, a black patent handbag and a dab of Joy perfume, I felt grown up and sophisticated. I was all of twenty-one, walking out of the hotel into the fresh spring air.

Jimmy and I were invited to see Peter Finch in "Two for the Seesaw" on the West End. After the play, Peter invited us to dine with him in SoHo. We had Japanese food, which I tried for the first time and found delicious.

During dinner, Peter had quite a bit to drink and his speech started to slur, until I could barely understand what he was saying. He started to recite a Keats poem but couldn't get the words out. Peter became so frustrated, he insisted we go back to his flat where he had a recording of himself reading the poem.

We took one of those snappy English cabs back to his flat, where he promptly placed a drink in Jimmy's hand and one in his own, then stumbled over to his tape recorder. After several false starts, he found the recording of the Keats poem. Unfortunately, he was as drunk and slurred on the tape as he had been in the restaurant.

A few days later, Peter's play ended and we all headed to Scotland to start shooting "Kidnapped."

Oh, Bonnie Scotland, home of my ancestor, Mary, Queen of Scots! Daddy had told me that we were directly related to Mary, Queen of Scots. His mother's name was Mary Stuart, and she might have been a lady-in-waiting for the royal family. True or not, I love the story.

We arrived to magical mists rolling over hills tinted with shades of lavender. A hotel on a Loch in Ballachulish would be our home during the filming. Jimmy asked that they wake us at 6:00 am on the first day of shooting. Both of us were surprised by a "wake-up" never to be forgotten. Sleeping next to Jimmy, who was curled up next to the wall, I was suddenly awakened with a very rude slap on my bottom.

"Wakey! Wakey!"

"Ow!" Rubbing my bottom, I turned over to see the flushed face of an older Scottish gent who had been sent as our wake-up call.

"Begging your pardon, Ma'am." He backed out of the room. Perhaps he thought he was slapping Jimmy. (In later years, we often woke our children with the cry of "Wakey, Wakey!")

Filming the interior scenes for "Kidnapped" took place at the Pinewood Studios, so we needed to rent a flat in London. That proved

Looking over a script in Scotland

to be difficult; people were hesitant to rent to us because we were so young. I went for an interview with a lady who had a lovely flat near the famous department store, Harrods. The flat was furnished in beautiful antiques and tiger and leopard rugs. Oh, how I wished she would lease it to us! I told her my husband was older, and we arranged for another meeting. Now what was I going to do?

I came up with a plan. At Harrods I bought a bowler hat and a proper Englishman's black umbrella. The next afternoon, Jim was dressed in a suit, the bowler hat, the umbrella on his arm, and a mustache the makeup man at the studio had artfully applied. We headed for our appointment.

The elegant landlady opened the door. On the way into the living room, I wasn't looking where I was going and had forgotten about the tiger rug in the foyer. My foot landed right in the tiger's mouth. While she took Jimmy down the hallway to show him the bedroom, I stayed behind and fought like a Roman gladiator, trying to extricate my foot.

When they came back, I had an innocent smile on my face and one tiger tooth behind my back. She indicated two gold chairs with satin seats. "Please do not sit on those, as they were from Buckingham Palace." When she turned away, I noticed a corner of Jim's mustache

London

coming loose. I quickly stuck it back on. The disguise worked. The flat was ours!

Walt Disney invited Jimmy and me to join other actors on a flight to Dublin for the opening night of "Darby O'Gill and the Little People." After the premiere, we were invited to a banquet, a formal affair at the Lord Mayor's mansion. We were both thrilled, but I had nothing to wear for such an occasion. Jimmy asked the studio if they had something in the wardrobe department I could borrow.

They were only too happy to act like fairy godmothers in the studio fitting room. They outfitted me in a dress once worn by Anne Heywood. A wardrobe mistress held the dress, and I carefully stepped into it, a beautiful yellow crepe gown, embroidered with pearls and topaz beads. It fit perfectly. I slipped on yellow satin shoes while the wardrobe mistress draped a white mink stole over my shoulders. (Fairy tales can come true.)

We boarded a private plane and flew to Dublin for a magical evening. When desserts were served, twenty waiters paraded them in on ice sculptures that were lit from beneath. Beautiful to see and delicious to eat!

One day, Jimmy surprised me with the idea of traveling to Russia before going to Tobago in the West Indies, where he had been asked to do another film for Disney, "Swiss Family Robinson." I thought it was a great idea. So my first flight on a jet airplane was aboard a Russian jet. The stewardesses served us gobs of caviar on dark brown bread. We visited Moscow, Kiev, and Leningrad, now St. Petersburg. What an adventure for two young people!

While Jim was filming for six months, we would live on an island in the West Indies. Both of us thought this would be a wonderful time to start our family. Jim wanted to start trying right away. So while we were in Russia, every night for a month, we tried to make a baby. The one night we skipped was after spending the whole day standing in line in Red Square, waiting to see Lenin and Stalin in their tombs. When we finally got inside, I saw a red light glowing over their bodies, as if they were under one of those red lights used in restaurants to keep food warm.

Back at the hotel that night, I begged, "Please, no baby-making tonight." I fell into bed exhausted. I didn't get pregnant.

Our first week in Tobago, we went to see the island doctor, an old boozy fellow. We told him how we had tried for a pregnancy and had only missed one night.

"That must have been the one night I could have gotten pregnant," I said.

He tipped his chair back and let out an uproarious laugh.

"You have to save up the sperm until just the right time." As he spoke the smell of rum wafted across the room. Looking at Jim, he winked and said, "It must have been a hell of a good month for you!"

After that, Jimmy saved up his sperm, I got some rest, and at just the right time we made love. Voilà—I was pregnant.

While in Tobago we became great friends with many wonderful people—John Mills and his wife, Mary, their daughters, Hayley and Juliette Mills, the lovely Dorothy McGuire and her husband, photographer John Swope, and best of all, Ken Annakin, the director of the film, and his charming English wife, Pauline. The Annakins became very close friends of ours; in the evenings we played Canasta together.

One night when Jimmy and I were winning, Ken, the famous, refined English director, swiped the cards off the table and onto the floor. Red in the face and furious because he was losing, he jumped up and down on the cards, while saying the most dreadful things. It was a sight to behold and really funny. We teased him about it till the day he died.

Jimmy was a different person when he was working. He didn't drink very much, and he was loving. Our time on the island was long but very pleasant. When I would feel woozy from the pregnancy, Pauline made me chicken sandwiches and gave me ginger ale. By the last month in Tobago, I was proudly showing a great big tummy and couldn't wait to get home so we could find a larger apartment with a special room for our baby.

On May 23, 1960, Charles Pennock MacArthur weighed in at eight pounds and three ounces. I was the smallest mother in New York City Hospital with the largest baby. But what a baby! He was beautiful. Charlie was named after Jimmy's father and my stepfather, Charles Pennock.

We alternated weekends with Mother and Dad on their farm in Bucks County and with Jim's Mom, (now "Mom" to me) in Nyack, proudly sharing our baby with his grandparents.

Lillian Gish, Grammy Helen, proud parents

Charlie was christened at St. Bartholomew's in New York City, where Lillian Gish went to church. She was one of Charlie's Godmothers, and Nell Rose, my friend, was his second Godmother. Eric Shaw, our very good friend from Solebury school days, was his Godfather.

When Charlie was just over a year, we spent a whole summer in Nyack. While we were there, Jimmy went to Hollywood for a few weeks to do another television show. When Jim came home, he acted noticeably different. He didn't really want to talk to me, but he wanted me by his side constantly. We stayed in the bedroom that had been his father's. There was a fireplace and a large desk in front of a bookcase packed with books. Oversized windows looked out over large oak trees and down to the Hudson River. Charlie slept in his crib in the room across the hall.

The first few nights that Jimmy was home from Hollywood, we made love almost every night. But something felt different to me. One night as I sat on the side of the bed, Jimmy got on his knees in front of me. He took both my hands in his and said he had something to tell me. He seemed nervous. "I'll understand if you want to divorce me." He looked down at the floor. I couldn't imagine what he was talking about. Then he slowly looked up.

"I was drunk and didn't know what I was doing."

On his recent trip he told me he had slept with someone and had become infected with a venereal disease. Since we had made love, the family doctor would be coming in the morning to give me a shot and some pills that I would have to take every four hours.

I had no words. I slowly reached for my robe. I moved as if in slow motion, in a dream state. Jim reached for me. I froze. He hugged me. I felt deadened, heavy, numb. Slowly, I found feeling in my feet. They moved, one foot in front of the other, slowly escaping from the person who moments ago had heard her husband tell of betrayal. That person had to be someone else, not me. I reached the doorway, put my hand on the doorframe to steady myself and walked slowly down the hallway to the staircase. Jimmy's words played over and over with each descending step.

"I was drunk-venereal disease- shots-pills-doctor."

What did he say it was, gonorrhea? When I reached the living room I started to shake uncontrollably, as if I might shake so hard I would break into pieces and die.

I stayed up all night looking out at the Hudson River. When the sun came up, I went back upstairs to check on Charlie. The doorbell rang; I heard the maid let the doctor in. He had come to the back door of the kitchen. I lifted Charlie out of his crib and carried him down to the kitchen, where I saw a black doctor's bag on the kitchen table.

Dr. Marchand stood beside the table. I mumbled a polite good morning and put Charlie in his highchair. We didn't talk. He gave me a shot, then handed me a bottle of pills.

"You must take one every four hours."

I was humiliated and ashamed. Charlie started to cry. I picked Charlie up and turned to say, "Thank you." I wanted to fall into the doctor's arms and cry. Instead, I looked at him and said goodbye.

Each time Jimmy took trips to Hollywood to make television appearances, I was never invited. He was a young, handsome actor with a roving eye and the burden of a young wife and baby. It proved to be a difficult challenge for Jim and our marriage.

Jim was offered another movie, "The Young Interns." He decided we should move to Hollywood. The idea frightened me, but I hoped that with Charlie and me along, perhaps Jim wouldn't be as tempted to stray. The last thing I wanted was a divorce. I didn't want to hurt Charlie the way I had been hurt as a child. And Helen, what would she think? I kept telling her how good a person Jim was. I had to try to make our marriage work, and maybe living together in Hollywood would give us this chance.

SIX

The Magic Kingdom and Sir Lancelot

Three days after Jimmy and I arrived in Los Angeles, I looked out the window of our hotel and saw red and orange flames leaping in the air. Most of Bel Air was on fire. Welcome to Los Angeles!

A few days later, my new agent in Hollywood, Ron DeBlasio at the William Morris Agency, asked me to audition for a role in the TV series, "Thriller," filming at Universal Studios. Jimmy hadn't started work yet and could look after Charlie while I auditioned. It was exciting to be asked to read for a role. I had a bit of that cocky "New York actor attitude," so superior to "Hollywood" actors. New York actors felt well trained, not just "pretty faces" who were able to say their lines over and over again on film, until they got it right. On stage, we had to get it right the first time!

Lucky me, I got the role and was put under contract. This was wonderful! I hadn't expected to find work right away. According to contract, I had to do a pilot once a year and star in eight shows for the studio. I was also allowed to work at other studios. It was the last of that kind of contract, and I was very fortunate to have that freedom.

Jim and I rented a Spanish-style house on Rodeo Drive in Beverly Hills and found a nanny for Charlie. She had been a nanny to Chris Robertson's children and came very highly recommended. Mae was just wonderful and I felt very secure leaving Charlie in her capable hands while I worked.

When Jim finished filming "The Young Interns," he was offered another film in the Philippines, starring Van Heflin. I couldn't go with him because I had to do a pilot. We decided I would join Jimmy after I finished shooting. Then we would cash in our first class tickets for tourist tickets (union rules required that the studio give us first class tickets) and go home by taking a route around the world.

When Jimmy left for location, I asked a good friend of mine, Lois Roberts, to stay with me. Luckily, we had twin beds in the master bedroom. Mae, our wonderful nanny, was in one bedroom and Charlie in the other. It was fun to have a friend stay with me. Lois was an actress too. I shared studio news with her while I was filming the pilot, "The First Hundred Years," about a student working his way through college while trying to support his wife and baby. Roger Perry was the young student and I played his wife.

One thing I shared with Lois was how much I liked Roger. He was such a good actor—charming, funny and very kind. I started to have the strangest feelings toward him. My heart beat faster as I anticipated going to work in the morning. I felt as if I really cared for him. Then I realized, of course I cared for him; he was playing a wonderful husband and father in the show. He was following a written script. Good husband, good father. After all, I didn't really know him. I liked him for the character he was playing. I did learn, as we talked between scenes, that he was the father of a three-year-old son named Chris. Roger

**"The First Hundred Years" with
Roger Perry and Nick Adams**

was separated from his wife and liked to spend as much time with Chris as he could.

One day I asked him if he thought it would be fun to bring Chris to the set when we were working on the back lot. I could ask Mae to pick up Chris and bring him along with Charlie, and we'd have a picnic with our boys during lunch break. He thought that would be great!

Roger really was a good father. He had such a way with his son, not harsh and controlling, but fun and loving. I couldn't help but compare him to Jimmy and the way Jim acted toward Charlie. Whenever Charlie touched something he shouldn't, Jim would slap his hand really hard. Charlie would touch it again and Jim would slap his little hand even harder. I would ask Jimmy not to do that, just remove Charlie or give him something else to play with. He'd say, "You don't know what you're talking about." Here was this grown man matching his will against a little boy. Charlie wouldn't cry, but I would.

By contrast, Roger was gentle with his son. We laughed and played with the two boys and had a good time. Oh dear, it wasn't just the role he was playing, he was a good father and my feelings started to mount and whirl and confuse me.

The weekend was coming. Roger asked me if I'd like to see a play on Sunday afternoon with him and the girl he was dating. "Oh, I think that would be very nice. Maybe afterwards you could pick up Chris and the three of you could come over for a barbeque at my house. Charlie and Chris could play together."

"Sure, that would be great," said Mr. Wonderful.

Sitting next to Roger and his date at the play was difficult. My shoulder touched his, and the warmth of his body gave me a feeling of never wanting to move. I held my hands tightly in my lap, afraid that I might reach out and put my hand on his. What in the world was going on with me? His girlfriend was very nice...... *and*...... I was married!

I was almost afraid to go to work. What if Roger could see how I felt? On the set, I couldn't look him in the eyes. Playing a scene with him was agony, because I had to look directly at him. I kept telling myself, "Be a good actress, Joyce. Just let him think you're acting when you have to look at him lovingly." Why did he seem to be looking at me the same way? Of course, he's a very good actor.

The producers called both of us into their office one day to tell us how pleased they were, what good work we were doing. They said the chemistry between us was just great on screen. A few days before we finished shooting, everyone was talking about a "wrap party" at the home of John Forsythe, one of the producers. As I was picking up my things and getting ready to go home, Roger asked me if he could take me to the wrap party. Of course he was just being polite. The leading man asking his leading lady was the correct thing to do. Even though I was married, I thought it would be all right, since he was a gentleman. My husband certainly went out with other women!

I couldn't wait to tell Lois that Roger had asked me to the party. I kept telling her about my feelings for Roger. I had to tell someone! What was I going to wear? How was I going to act? Act is the operative word. I certainly couldn't let him know how I felt. Be cool. Be lady-like. I decided to wear a pink dress and carry a pink chiffon scarf for my hair.

The doorbell rang. There was Roger, ever so handsome. I tried to act very nonchalant, though my knees felt weak as I walked down the path to his car. His white Oldsmobile convertible with red leather interior looked like Cinderella's royal coach to me. Roger gallantly opened the car door for me.

We stayed at the party only a short time before Roger asked if I'd like to drive to the beach. I thought a drive certainly couldn't be a bad thing to do. With the top of the convertible down and my scarf secured, we drove to the beach. My scarf was the only thing that felt secure; my insides were shaky. I kept repeating my mantra, "Be cool, be lady-like, this is only a drive to the beach."

We went to The Point, a restaurant overlooking the ocean. The hostess led us to a table by the fireplace. Roger pulled my chair out for me, and I sat watching the flames dance back and forth. I turned to look at the ocean. Lights from the restaurant were shining on the whitecaps. The waves pounded against the shore and my heart pounded in my chest.

The waitress came to our table. Roger asked what I would like to drink. I didn't really drink very much. Occasionally I would have a Dubonnet before dinner when Jimmy and I visited my parents at the farm. In the most sophisticated voice I could summon, I said, "May I please have a Dubonnet on the rocks with a twist of lemon." Roger asked if I had ever had it with gin. Wow! That sounded pretty strong, but maybe it would help my nervousness. Also, I wanted to sound experienced. Most of all I wanted to please Roger, so a Dubonnet with gin it was.

Roger talked and I listened. Or rather I tried to listen, but I was too nervous to have any idea what he was saying. I just thought he was wonderful. I nervously folded the napkin back and forth and occasionally took little sips of my drink.

During the ride home along Sunset Boulevard I was very quiet. As we got closer to my house, my heart started to pound again. Would he kiss me goodnight? I hoped so. Roger parked the car and came around to open the door for me. He gently took my hand, walked me to the door, thanked me for letting him take me to the party, and left.

My heart sank. Was he just being polite, taking his leading lady to the party and the beach? I told myself to stop this foolish feeling. In the morning I should start packing and get ready to join Jimmy in the Philippines.

The next night, Lois and I were sound asleep when the doorbell rang. I looked at the clock. It was three in the morning! I don't know why, maybe wishful thinking, I said, "I bet it's Roger."

I grabbed my robe, ran a brush through my hair, pinched my cheeks for color, and ran downstairs. I looked through the peephole and saw those beautiful blue eyes, a little bloodshot at this time of the morning. I opened the door to a swaying Roger, with one hand behind his back.

"I was just in the neighborhood and wondered if you might have some coffee to go with this chocolate cake?" From behind his back, out came a Canter's pastry box. I think he needed the help of a few stiff drinks to arrive at my front door at three o'clock in the morning.

I didn't care how he got there; I was just happy he was there. I laughed to myself as I led him into the kitchen. He sat at the table and watched me make a pot of coffee. I poured coffee and we poured our hearts out to each other.

During the wee hours of the morning, Roger told me he had been put up for adoption when he was two years old. I told him I had been in foster homes because my mother had to work. He was sad his marriage hadn't worked out and he was separated from his wife and son. I told him I was sad because my husband not only had affairs, but he was unkind to me and Charlie. I said I didn't know what to do, but I didn't want to get divorced. My mother and father were divorced and it had been very painful for me as a child. I didn't want Charlie to experience that.

It wasn't until the sun came up that we stopped talking. A strong bond developed between Roger and me over chocolate cake and coffee. I realized that I had fallen in love with this man and could do nothing about it. I didn't know how he felt about me, except I felt he liked me and trusted me as a friend. At the front door Roger and I hugged goodbye. I watched him walk to his car. As I closed the door, I knew I must close the door to my feelings for Roger.

I went upstairs to get Charlie. I fed him breakfast and hugged him tight. The next day I would leave for the Philippines and I wouldn't see Charlie for several weeks.

Charlie's second birthday would arrive while I were gone. I was going to miss him so much. Although I knew he would be in very capable hands, it would still be hard for me. But I thought I must go, to try to keep my marriage together.

Early the next day I boarded a plane to fly to the Philippines. Once I sat down and buckled my seat belt, my thoughts returned to Roger. I tried to stop thinking about him and our late-night conversation in the kitchen, but I couldn't. What if the pilot for our show didn't sell? I would never see him again! But if it did sell, how would I keep my feelings in check? Weary and lacking sleep, I soon drifted off.

We landed first in Hawaii, then Guam and finally Manila. The plane was taking me farther and farther away from Roger. I felt as if my insides were being emptied out, like a glass of wine that had tipped over. It was a feeling of indescribable emptiness. I was being the good wife. But was I? These feelings I had for Roger were wrong. How do you make feelings go away? I hoped when I saw Jimmy everything would be all right, and I could start to forget how much I had grown to care for Roger.

When the plane landed in Manila, I stepped out into air that was hot and sticky. Someone from the film crew met me and took me to the hotel where Jim and the other actors were staying. After helping me with my luggage, he explained that they wouldn't finish shooting until late that night. I asked him to please take me to location. He looked hesitant, but agreed. I thought the sooner I could see Jimmy and put my arms around him, the sooner I could fill that feeling of emptiness.

Halfway to location, we stopped and took a jeep and then an oxcart. I knew I was going to surprise Jimmy; he thought I'd be waiting at the hotel for him. When I saw him in the distance, I jumped out of the cart and ran full speed toward him. With my arms open, ready to hug and kiss him, he stopped me short. He put his hands up.

"Don't kiss me here, the natives won't understand."

I understood. He was more than likely having an affair with one of the natives and had forgotten to mention me. I hoped I was wrong, but I doubted it. After shooting that day, I drove back to the hotel with Jimmy. I sat silently as he chatted away with the other actors and crew members about the day's shoot. We arrived at the hotel and went up to our room. Jimmy opened the door, shoved me down on the bed, lay on top of me and said, "I want to fuck you."

I felt totally empty, just an outer shell. No feeling… no pain.

The rest of the time in the Philippines was difficult. I missed Charlie terribly and couldn't get Roger out of my mind. Some days I went on location with Jimmy and brooded. It was hot, sticky, and miserable. We were carefully guarded on some locations because of the guerilla warriors who lived in the hills. Our guards carried guns. The situation was unnerving.

One day on a beach location, I was lying in a Nipa Hut trying to read. I put my book down and looked up at the roof made of palm fronds and stared at the bamboo walls. There wasn't the slightest breeze. My perspiration dripped onto the pages of the book. There wasn't a book in the world that could take my mind off Roger. I felt miserable and sorry for myself. I thought it best to try and shape up, get over this mooning around! I decided to take a walk along the ocean.

As I was walking and cooling my feet in the water, I had a feeling I was being followed. I turned around and saw a man, who stopped. I walked again. He walked. I stopped, looked behind. He stopped. Frightened, I quickened my steps and he quickened his. I saw a family picnicking on the beach and ran toward them and sat right down with them. The man who had been following me ran towards where I was sitting with the family of strangers. I could see that he had a gun. Nervously, I told the family I was sorry to intrude and hoped that the man following me would go away. Instead, he came right up to me.

"I've been told to bring you back to the set. It is too dangerous for you to be walking alone. Please come back with me now."

He was one of the guards from location. I was so relieved. I apologized to the family and left. At that time, if you went to a movie in the Philippines, you would see a sign in the box office window, CHECK YOUR GUNS.

When Jim's film was completed, we boarded a plane for the first leg of our "around the world" trip. Of course, in the Philippines, we were already half way around. We went to Hong Kong, Thailand, India, Egypt, Greece, and Paris. Our good friend, Eric Shaw, met us in Paris. Now that filming and most of our travels were completed, Jimmy started to drink again, heavily. I had hoped that the romance of Paris would once again bring us close. But instead, Jimmy was too hung over and wanted to sleep most of the day. So during the day Eric showed me the sights of Paris and at night Jimmy would join us and we'd all go out. And the drinking would begin again.

At last, we arrived back home in Beverly Hills. Sweeping Charlie up in my arms, hugging him tight and kissing his chubby little cheeks made me so happy. It was too long to be away from my little one. I was glad to be home, but when I went into the kitchen and saw the table where Roger and I had sat together, my heart sank.

The pilot Roger and I shot was not picked up for a series. It was important for me to get on with my life and get Roger out of my mind, and my heart.

Jimmy and I decided to buy a house, so every day I set out with a realtor. When I suggested to her that we look in the San Fernando Valley instead of Beverly Hills, she was shocked. "You must live in Beverly Hills. The valley just isn't the proper place for you."

I had no idea what she was talking about. It was much less expensive than Beverly Hills and seemed somehow more real. To me, from the East Coast, Beverly Hills seemed like fantasy land. I thought if you looked behind the great big houses with perfectly manicured lawns, you'd see that there was no back, just slats of lumber holding them up, like the make-believe houses on the back lots of studios.

One day a realtor and I drove up a driveway lined with trees, their branches hanging with beautiful purple flowers. At the end of the driveway was an absolutely charming home, modeled after an English carriage house. It was perfect! The house was made of fieldstone, very much like the houses in Bucks County where Jimmy and I had gone to school. There were two patios, a fireplace in the living room and master bedroom, three bedrooms, walnut floors throughout, and a guesthouse for our housekeeper. It also had an orchard in the back yard and a big oak tree in the front yard for Charlie to climb. Oh, how I hoped Jimmy would like the house! And I had a plan.

The next day I asked the realtor to show Jimmy three ugly houses we had seen, about the same price as the carriage house. I asked her to save the English Carriage house for last. I told Jimmy that I had found four houses and he could choose which one he liked the best. The first three houses went from bad to worse. One house had gold specks in the stucco, and another had Greek statues surrounding the swimming pool. When Jimmy saw the first houses, he was polite and didn't hurt my feelings. However, he said he kind of liked the house with the Greek statues. I thought, what have I done? What if he really likes that one?

Driving up to the English carriage house, my heart was in my throat. He fell in love with it at first sight. We moved in four weeks later.

A short time after we were settled in our new home, I was cast as a murder suspect on the "Perry Mason Show." Raymond Burr was ill at the time, and the very distinguished Walter Pidgeon was guest starring as the defense attorney.

Late one morning, while we were in the middle of a courtroom scene, Barbara Hale, who played Della Street, Mason's secretary, was seated next to me. Mr. Pidgeon, playing my attorney, was cross-examining an actor on the witness stand. While the cameras were rolling, suddenly a stagehand burst through the courtroom doors and shouted,

"The President has been shot!"

On the set of "Perry Mason" with Charlie, Walter Pidgeon and Jim

I remember that moment so well, just as everyone does who first heard the news. Barbara and I both said, "Oh God!" Our heads went down in disbelief and shock. The director said, "Let's all take a break." Everyone rushed to the phones to call loved ones. There was an immediate need to be in touch with family. As Jimmy and I talked, I sobbed into the phone. Mr. Pidgeon, seeing how upset I was, asked if he could take me to lunch. We ate silently. He put his large hand over mine; I think he was trying to give both of us courage. When I left the studio that night, a light rain was falling. It was as if the angels in heaven were crying.

✳

The next week, while I was still working on the Perry Mason Show, my agent called. "How would you like to do a television special with Fred Astaire?"

"Who wouldn't?"

"Well, Universal wants you to play opposite him in a special."

"Oh sure, right, what's up?"

"I'm serious."

"Ron, that's every woman's dream. Don't tease."

"I'm not. Now what's your answer?"

"You really are serious? Fred Astaire?"

"Yes."

"Oh, Ron, I've dreamed of dancing with Fred Astaire! My mother and I used to go from one end of New York City to the other just looking for his old movies." My mother used to take me to every Trans-Lux Theater, where they played "Top Hat," "Swing Time," all the old ones. When I was told I'd get to dance with Fred Astaire, I was speechless. Dancing with Fred Astaire!

Ron teased, "Should I tell them you're not interested?"

"Don't you dare!" I couldn't wait to tell Jimmy. Not only was I going to play opposite Fred Astaire, but there was a scene where we would dance together. When I told Jimmy he said, "First Ginger, then Rita, now Joyce."

The first day of rehearsals I was so nervous. I didn't want to seem anxious and arrive too early. I certainly didn't want to be unprofessional and arrive late, so I arrived 45 minutes early and sat in the ladies' room, studying the script and checking my watch every five minutes. At three minutes to nine, I walked out of the ladies' room, down the hallway to the rehearsal room, and opened the door a crack to peep in. I saw him—Fred Astaire! Debonair in white trousers, with a silk tie for a belt, he was the image of undeniable grace and confidence. I shut the door and stood for a moment, trying to catch my heart before it blew right out of my chest. Slowly I opened the door a crack. He looked at me and with his index finger, beckoned me to enter.

But when we started rehearsal, I found out it wasn't going to be a beautiful waltz, with him lifting me into the air the way he danced with Ginger Rogers, but no! It was the twist, of all things! He pulled me aside behind one of the flats onstage.

"Joyce, dear, I don't know the twist, could you teach it to me?"

"Oh, Mr. Astaire, oh my goodness, you want *me* to teach you a dance?!"

"Yes, and you'd better do it quickly, because it's in the next scene."

I was astonished, but he was older and didn't do the modern dances. So I took him behind the flat and showed him how to do the twist, and then we danced it, for Alcoa Presents, on TV. (The whole episode of "Mr. Lucifer" from Fred Astaire's Alcoa Premiere Theatre is on You Tube, twist and all.) Just to watch the man walk across the floor—he didn't walk, he glided.

He was having trouble with his lines and I felt so bad for him. We kept having to do it over and over. He apologized to me!

Dancing with Fred Astaire

"You poor girl, having to do this so many times."

"Oh, Mr. Astaire, it's the thrill of my life!"

I was too intimidated to ask him to have lunch with us. When I acted with him in that show, he was playing the devil and Elizabeth Montgomery was the naughty secretary. I was the goody-two-shoe wife. Elizabeth was trying to tempt my husband and Fred Astaire was trying to tempt me. (He could have tempted me any time in real life!) Elizabeth was such a good actress and very fun. She was wearing a bikini in one scene. I don't know what got into me—one day I got a banana and put cold cream on it and stuck it down the back of her bikini! We had so much fun, fooling around. Who would imagine that years later I would end up being the stepmother to her children?

A couple of years later, I was dancing at a charity ball in Beverly Hills when someone tapped my partner on the shoulder and cut in. My new partner took me in his arms and said, "You may not remember me. My name is Fred Astaire."

Can you imagine? What a humble, sweet, and wonderful person.

At home one morning, Jimmy awoke with a very swollen, frightful-looking eye. His eyeball was actually bulging out. After several tests at the eye doctor's office, the doctor said he didn't understand why this was happening and wanted to schedule exploratory surgery. He would enter near Jim's temple to see what was causing the swelling, which continued to get worse.

Both Helen and I begged him to get a second opinion before submitting to such a dangerous procedure, but Jim absolutely insisted that he go ahead with the surgery. Three days before the procedure, the surgeon's nurse called to tell us the doctor was ill with the flu and had to cancel the surgery until a later date. Mom and I were so relieved.

A few days later, Jimmy traveled to New York to meet with Dr. Marchand, the family doctor. Within hours Dr. Marchand had Jim with a specialist, who diagnosed a growth behind Jim's eye caused from a childhood injury. When Jim was nine, Footie and he had been taking golf clubs and hitting the heads off flowers in the garden. Footie, on his back swing, hit Jimmy right above the eye. Surgery was scheduled.

Helen was out of town in a play but arranged to take the train into New York the morning of the surgery. It was a very serious operation. The night before the surgery the doctor came in to speak with Jimmy and me. He told us that Jim had a fifty-fifty chance of making it. He explained the procedure. "First I make an incision across the top of the head, then I will fold down the skin of the forehead, cut a window in a section of the skull above the eye, drain the brain fluid, and then cut out the mass behind the eye. Then I put everything back in place. Are there any questions?"

Jim answered bravely, "I understand."

One thought played in my mind. There was a chance he wouldn't make it.

The doctor left the room. I lay down next to Jimmy on his hospital bed. In silence we held hands and looked at a picture of Charlie that I had propped up on the table at the end of his bed. The nurse came in and gave Jim a sleeping pill.

I held his hand until he fell asleep. After a while the nurse tiptoed in and motioned for me to follow her to a bed where I could spend the night. I wanted to be up at six in the morning to be with Jimmy before he went into surgery. Helen planned to be there too.

I hardly slept. I kept looking at my watch. At dawn, I dressed quickly and went to Jim's room. I saw that his bed was gone. The space where his bed had been was empty, with only a lonely pair of his bedroom slippers. I panicked.

I ran down the hall to the nurse's station to ask where Jimmy was. She said they had taken him into surgery earlier than expected. I sat and waited, my hands folded in prayer. I stared at the slippers, and waited for Helen. I was frightened and agitated. Why didn't she take an earlier train? Why wasn't she here?

An hour later she arrived with Lucy Kroll, her agent. Tears flowing, I leaped up and hugged her tight. After trying to comfort me, she and Lucy suggested we go to the cafeteria for some breakfast. The last thing I could think of was eating.

In the cafeteria my thoughts were in the operating room. Mom and Lucy chatted about costumes for the show Mom was doing. I wanted to talk about Jimmy. Maybe they were keeping up a happy chatter to distract me, but all I could think about was what was happening several floors above us in the operating room.

The operation was successful! After a week in the hospital we went to the farm for Jimmy to get more rest. Finally Jimmy, Charlie and I flew home.

*

Back in Hollywood I did guest appearances on different TV shows, including a lot of Westerns at Universal, including "The Virginian," "Destry Rides Again," "Laramie," and "Wagon Train." One day when I was headed for the commissary, dressed in a period costume for "Wagon Train," I saw a familiar face on the other side of the street—Roger Perry.

It had been a few years since I had last seen him, at least in person; Roger was often in my dreams. I was surprised and very happy to see him. My heart pumped faster, with that old strange feeling again.

"Hello there," he said, waving from across the street.

"Hello," I said, careful not to reveal my deepest feelings.

He crossed the street and started talking as if no time had passed since we had last seen each other. If he only knew that he had been in my thoughts as I traveled around the world! When I had seen the Taj Mahal by moonlight I wept, thinking of him. Jimmy had asked what was wrong. I said the beauty of the building made me cry.

Roger's voice was music to my ears. He told me he was shooting a new series on Stage 15, "Arrest and Trial." I told him I was going to do a series, "Tom, Dick and Mary."

"Well, I guess we'll be seeing each other." Why did he have to be so handsome? And those eyes, those beautiful blue eyes.

"I hope so," I said. I wondered if he knew just how much I hoped to see him again.

A week later I started filming "Tom, Dick and Mary." I played Mary. Don Galloway played my husband Tom, and Steve Franken played Dick, a young doctor who lived with us. We were shooting on Stage 16, next to Stage 15.

Jimmy wasn't working very much. He was waiting and hoping for the next film to come along. This wasn't good because when he wasn't working, he drank. Times at home were not happy, but I tried to bury my unhappiness in work.

When I returned home at night I would give Charlie a bath, tuck him into bed, and sing songs to him. On the weekends we would play together and go on outings. He was my joy in life.

Sometimes at work, I would see Roger come over to our stage. I hoped that he was coming to say hello to me. Instead, he would give me a casual, "Hello, I just came by to see a friend who's working on your show."

That "Hello" fell right into my heart.

I often visited the stage Roger was working on. Of course I went to see Roger.

"The coffee is so much better on your set, I just came over to get a cup."

We always had an excuse for appearing on each other's sets. We never said we were there to see each other—we knew.

At home one night I got a call from my agent. "Joyce, they want you to guest star in 'Arrest and Trial.' It starts shooting next week on location in Vegas. It's a great role. Shall I tell them you'll do it?"

Oh my, location in Vegas, and Roger one of the leading actors? My mind raced.

"Well?"

"Oh, yes, of course. That's great."

"OK, they want you for wardrobe fittings on Monday. They'll give you a call."

I hung up and looked over at Jimmy, on the sofa strumming his guitar.

"Jimmy, that was my agent. They want me to go to Vegas to film at the end of next week. It's a really good role."

Not taking his eyes off his guitar, he said, "Great."

"You'll go with me, right?"

"Nah, I don't want to go."

"Jimmy, I really want you to."

"Well, I don't feel like it."

"Jimmy, I need you to go with me."

"I told you, no."

It was then I made the mistake of telling him about my feelings for Roger.

"Remember, when you had the affair? The one you had to tell me about because I had to take pills." Still he made no eye contact. Didn't raise his head to look at me, just kept playing that dumb guitar.

"Roger Perry and I did a show together, the one that was a pilot for a series. I liked him a lot, I even thought I might be in love with him."

Still no response.

"It was all because I was hurt and he was so kind. Please come with me, I don't want to be in Vegas without you."

He raised his head and looked at me. "I don't care."

I asked my friend Barb to go with me. "Barb, you have to go. I don't want to be tempted. Just don't leave my side."

Some days I had shown up when she was teaching art class and stood forlornly in the doorway until she could come and talk to me. She listened to the same old weepy story about Roger over and over again. Luckily, she said she would go to Vegas.

We no sooner stepped through the door of the Sands Hotel than Roger appeared.

"Hi there! Listen, I heard you were doing the show so I got tickets for the theater here at the hotel tonight. Would you like to go to dinner and the show?"

Was he kidding? Would I like to go? Of course I would like to go! As casually as I could, I said, "Oh, Roger, that is so nice of you, but I don't want to leave my friend."

"Not a problem, I'll get her a date so we can all go together."

"That would be so nice."

Roger and I sat next to each other, chatting away, oblivious to Barb and her date across the table. When the show started, Roger reached for my hand under the table. What a lovely sensation, holding hands with this man I thought about constantly. I looked at him shyly and he squeezed my hand.

After the show, Barb leaned over to say, "We'll be right back, we're just going to gamble for a while." Panic-stricken, I whispered, "Don't leave me, please." She paid no attention and off she went.

Roger suggested we go see a lounge show and have a drink. The lounge show consisted of a couple in scanty costumes performing a very sensual dance. Roger ordered me a Harvey Wallbanger, a popular drink at that time. I sipped on it as we watched the dancers rub up and down each other's bodies. My Wallbanger was disappearing quickly, and all I could think about was banging. I mean, having a banger, a Harvey Wallbanger. It was really time to leave! Thanks to the drinks and the dance, I was turned on. A voice inside said, "Let's get out of here! And I mean now!"

Just then Roger said, "I guess we should go. We both have to work tomorrow." I gathered my purse and tried desperately to listen to my inner voice: "Go to your room."

Ooops! We walked right past my room to his. If only the feeling of the Wallbanger and the "I want to make love to you" feeling would just go away.

Roger opened the door to his room, took me by the hand and led me to his bed. I sat down at the foot of the bed and Roger, ever so gently, put his arm around me and lowered me on the bed. He leaned down to kiss me, and just as his lips were about to reach mine, I sat up abruptly and said, "I'm so sorry, I can't do this!" I got to the door and closed it behind me.

The next day I didn't see Roger. I wanted to tell him how sorry I was, how much I cared for him. But he finished his scenes and took an early plane back to L.A.

*

One night Jimmy came home about four in the morning. I was sound asleep. I had to get up early the next day for work. Jimmy, in a drunken state, climbed under the covers at the bottom of the bed, pulled on my foot and yanked it as hard as he could. I screamed! He frightened me to death!

He laughed, got into bed next to me and grabbed my breast. It was better not to try to fight him off. If I did, he would just become enraged and things would turn worse. When he became angry, he would sometimes twist the skin under my arm. I bit my lip and endured his bitter breath as he forced himself on me. While he took pleasure in destroying my soul, tears of anger rolled down my face.

The next day, in my dressing room trailer outside stage 16, I wondered how I could go home to another night of drinking and pretending that things were all right.

There was a knock on the door.

"Joyce are you there?" It was Roger. Maybe Roger was coming to tell me that he loves me, that I can leave Jimmy. We'll get married and everything will be fine.

"Yes, I'm here."

"Can I come in? I have something to tell you."

With a wide grin he said, "Congratulate me!"

"Congratulations." I realized he wasn't there to carry me off on a white horse.

"I'm going to have a baby." He searched my eyes for my reaction.

"Oh, that's wonderful," I said through a tight smile. "You went back to your wife?"

"Yes, I just wanted you to know."

"Thank you, that's great, I'm very happy for you." Another forced smile.

"Well, I have to get back to my set. I just wanted you to know."

He left and my heart went with him. I cried so hard, mascara ran down my face. Suddenly I realized I was ruining my makeup and the makeup man would be upset with me. I tried to stop crying, but I couldn't. I leaned over so the tears would fall on the floor instead of running down my face.

I wondered why he had come to tell me. Were my feelings towards him not as hidden as I thought? Was this his way of telling me he knew how I felt, that I must not feel that way? Why did I have the feeling that he was really coming to see me when he came to our set? It must have been wishful thinking.

SEVEN

My Mary

I t was easier to go home in the evenings when Jimmy wasn't there. He was in London doing a film with Richard Widmark, "The Bedford Incident." A few weeks after Jimmy left for England, my show was cancelled. Charlie and I packed up and flew to London to be with Jimmy. It seemed that every time my career was on the move, so was I, always off to locations to be with my husband. I believed that as much as I loved acting, family came first. I also thought if Roger can have a baby, so can I. Jimmy thought it was a splendid idea. Because he was working, he wasn't drinking as much. He was being loving and caring again, so it was the right time.

We had a lovely stay in London in our little flat. Not as elegant as the first flat we had rented when Jimmy was filming "Kidnapped," but it was good for Charlie with a park right across the street. Christmas was coming. One day I dragged a huge tree up to our flat and bought a turkey that was too fat to fit into our tiny oven. We invited Brad Dillon and Peter Graves for Christmas dinner. They were in the film and couldn't be with their families for the holidays, so I wanted to create a nice Christmas for everyone. Santa brought Charlie a knight's costume and a castle to play with. On Boxing Day, the day after Christmas, we went to visit our friends, Pauline and Ken Annakin, in the country. It was nice to get out of town and enjoy the delicious dinner Pauline prepared.

After a month, I thought I might be pregnant. I visited the doctor to see what the rabbit would say, pregnant or not pregnant? In those days the pregnancy test was called a rabbit's test. I imagined a doctor pulling a rabbit out of a tall silk hat and the rabbit, looking like Bugs Bunny, would have a sign saying "Yes!" or "No."

Pauline and I were shopping in Fortnum and Mason and stopped in their tea room. I was to call the doctor to find out what the rabbit said. I took the elevator to the floor with the telephone booths and placed a call to the doctor.

"Congratulations," came the English accent, "you're with child."

In a daze, I rode up and down the elevator several times until a sweet Cockney accent jogged me back to reality.

"I say, Love, which floor did you want?"

Looking back over my shoulder, I stepped out of the elevator and said with a big grin, "I'm going to have a baby!"

A few months later, Jimmy, Charlie and I were off to Segovia, Spain, where Jim was filming "Battle of the Bulge," directed by Ken Annakin. Henry Fonda was in the cast, along with Robert Shaw and Telly Savalas.

We rented a charming cottage just outside the grounds of the Royal Palace in Segovia. Jim rose early to go on location, and shortly afterwards Charlie and I would trundle off downstairs to greet the sweet lady who took care of the cottage. After we settled in front of the fireplace, she would bring us freshly-squeezed blood orange juice, farm eggs, and peasant bread toasted with swirls of sweet butter and marmalade. To top it off, hot chocolate for Charlie and tea for me. Charlie and I spent mornings in front of the fireplace doing his lessons. I taught him numbers by playing cards with him, and we practiced writing letters of the alphabet. Thank heaven he was too young for spelling, or we both would have been in trouble, due to my dyslexia. Mark Twain said, "Never trust a man who can only spell a word one way," but dyslexia caused me serious problems.

Young Charlie in Spain

Henry and Shirley Fonda became our good friends during the filming. We knew Hank's daughter, Jane Fonda, from Jim's days on Broadway. On Hank's birthday, we invited Ken and Pauline for a birthday dinner at our home. I found out that Hank, more than anything, longed for corned beef hash and Jell-O. Can you imagine? But in Spain, on location, this would be a treat for him.

To jazz up the Jell-O, I put chopped bits of fruit and nuts into the gelatin. Hank seemed pleased with his birthday dinner. Now for the big surprise, his birthday dessert. After we all sang "Happy Birthday," I presented the Jell-O mold and served everyone. As soon as Hank dug in and put a mouthful of Jell-O in his mouth, Shirley yelled, "No, no! Don't do it, don't do it! Spit it out!"

I was horrified. Hank put the spoon down and spit out the Jell-O. Shirley said, "Oh my God, it has apples in it!"

I asked Hank, "Don't you like apples?"

"I'm highly allergic. I could die if I eat one."

Thank heaven I didn't kill Henry Fonda on his birthday!

On the Pyrenees Mountains between Segovia and Madrid, Charlie donned his first pair of skis. One snowy day I was watching Charlie ski. While Jimmy was filming "Battle of the Bulge" I was very pregnant, battling my own bulge. As I watched Charlie I suddenly became very dizzy and fainted in the snow. Was I ever lucky! Hank came along and rescued me, even though I had almost killed him with Jell-O.

This was an exceptionally happy and good time for Jimmy and me, as he hardly ever drank when he was shooting. We moved to an apartment in Madrid where the interior scenes for the film were being shot. Jimmy and I both loved flamenco music and dancing, so after tucking Charlie into bed and telling our babysitter to keep a close watch on him, we spent some evenings listening to flamenco. Jimmy started to take his guitar playing seriously. Often I would see him practice by strumming his fingers on a table or his knee. I prayed this happy time would last.

When we arrived back in Los Angeles, I had only one month before the baby was due. Helen came to California to stay with us and welcome her new grandchild into the world. The night before the baby came, she and I went to see "The Sound of Music."

Because I was two weeks late, the doctor wanted to induce labor. The next evening Jimmy, Helen and I sat in the maternity ward of St. John's Hospital in Santa Monica playing Perquackey, a board game. You had to spell words from letters you spilled out of a little cup. Every once in a while, I would have a severe labor pain. Jim and Mom turned pale. I panted to relieve the labor pain, then nonchalantly continued the game. It was the only time I ever won a spelling game.

On September 4, 1965, Mary Hayes MacArthur weighed in at seven pounds and six ounces. I watched the birth and then the doctor

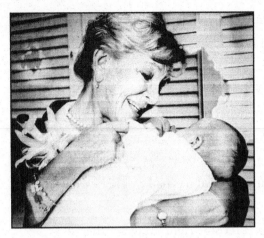
Grammy Helen and baby Mary

laid her on my chest. She was all gray and not breathing. The doctor put his hand on her little chest and pushed gently. The most beautiful sound was that little being coming to life. She let out the sweetest cry and turned pink. As I lay on the gurney being pushed to my room, I could hear the wheels turning, and with each turn I said, "It's a girl, it's a girl!"

Charlie loved his new baby sister. When he came home from school I would try not to be nursing so Charlie would have my undivided attention. But one day Mary slept late and when she awoke, she was starving. I was lying in bed nursing Mary when Charlie came home. He climbed onto the bed, watched her nursing for a moment, then he came very close to my other breast and asked, "Whatcha got in this one?" I think he was hoping for lemonade.

One night we had a party for Ken Annakin, who had just completed writing and directing "The Magnificent Men and Their Flying Machines." The valet parking attendants were dressed in jodhpurs, old leather pilot helmets and silk scarves around their necks. I made the red, white, and blue flower arrangements and put a little English and French flag in each arrangement. My friend Barbara made paper maché flying balloons that hung at different heights overhead. Guests danced under the stars while an orchestra played beneath the sprawling oak tree. Nancy Sinatra, Connie Stevens, James Franciscus, Jim Stacey, Rona Barrett, Nick Adams, Dorothy Maguire, Telly Savalas,

Lee Marvin, and many other Hollywood friends came to meet Ken and celebrate his successful film. It was great fun and an elegant evening, if I say so myself.

That summer, Jim and I took six-year-old Charlie and nine-month-old Mary to Chicago, where Jim and I were starring in "John Loves Mary" at the Pheasant Run Theater. One night after our performance, the phone rang in our hotel suite. It was Mother.

"Try not to be upset, but your Dad has had a mild heart attack and is in the hospital."

My heart was pounding. "I'll come right away, Mother."

"No, I may need you more later, and you must do the play."

Late after Sunday night's performance, I decided to fly just for the day to see Dad. As I was leaving the hotel room, I looked at Mary asleep in her crib. "Jim, I think I'll take Mary. She'll help cheer up Mother and Dad, and I need her."

Mary slept soundly on my lap all the way to Philadelphia. A friend of Mother's picked us up at the airport in the early morning and drove us to the hospital. Dad, handsome as ever in blue silk pajamas, sat up in bed and reached for Mary. I placed her in his arms. I noticed that Mother had brought the bed linens and their china from home for Dad, to make his hospital stay more comfortable.

Dad's chubby granddaughter nestled close to him was the best medicine in the world. When it was time for us to leave, I stood with Mary in my arms at the door. Dad said, "I just want to live long enough for her to know I'm her grandfather."

"Dad, don't you dare let anything happen to you!" Indicating Mother, I asked playfully, "What would I do with her?" I thought Mother's world would come to an end without her Charles.

"I love you Dad. Get well."

Dad was improving and due home in time for their tenth wedding anniversary. I was relieved. Mother bought new outdoor furniture to surprise him. "Now when your Dad comes home, we'll be able to sit together outside at sunset and watch the deer graze in the meadows."

Jim and I drove from Chicago back to California in our new station wagon. On Mother and Dad's anniversary I called from our motel room in Price, Utah. Mother answered. I said, "Happy anniversary! I'll bet you're glad to have Dad home."

"Is Jim with you, honey?" Her voice sounded strained.

"Yes, he is. Is something wrong?"

"Joyce, honey, your Dad passed away. We had no way to reach you, so we postponed the funeral. I knew that you would call on our anniversary. Now listen carefully, we have two airline tickets waiting for you in Los Angeles for tomorrow night. It's the only way you can get here in time for the funeral."

"Don't worry, we'll leave right now and drive through the night. I love you."

I sat down on the bed. I loved this man so much. My body felt heavy, as if I might sink right through the floor. Too numb for tears, I felt as if I were sinking, melting away, but I had to be strong for Mother. I had to pull the family together and get to California in a hurry so we could fly to Philadelphia.

Jimmy had driven all day to Price, Utah. He was much too tired to drive any further, so I drove through Bryce Canyon on the darkest night of my life. My young cousin, Linda, was with us. She had come to visit and was helping with the children. Jimmy, Charlie and Mary were asleep in the back of the car. Linda sat in the front seat and kept me going all through the night, feeding me chocolate chip cookies and coffee. My eyes felt like sandbags, and I barely made it into Las Vegas before waking Jim to drive the next five hours.

When we arrived home, my two best friends, Barbara and Peggy, were waiting for me. On the coffee table in our living room was a bright bouquet of flowers with a note that read, "Love to my brave girl, Mom."

In Philadelphia, the chapel of the funeral home was packed. Mother always dressed impeccably, but today she wore an old discolored white suit, and it looked as if she had taken scissors to her short curly black hair. I was very concerned; she didn't seem at all like herself. Later she told me she wore that suit because she wanted to wear something she would never wear again. She wanted to burn it.

There was a small reception at the farm with close friends. I left the gathering and went out to the field of peonies where Dad and I had spent many hours picking and gathering flowers. He taught me to pick them when they were just about to open. Then we would grade the flowers and put them in buckets of water to take to his store. His employees teased him, "Look, the boss is growing his own flowers."

Sitting in the dirt between rows of peonies, I remembered the wonderful times Dad and I shared. Dad teaching me to waltz, Dad coming to see me perform, Dad telling his silly jokes, Dad waltzing with Mother on their wedding day. I pictured him on his tractor tending flowers. I could hear him say, "Don't just talk theater—it's boring to others. Learn about everything." Each memory brought a wave of new tears.

It was difficult to leave Mother, but the children were waiting for us at home, and she had friends nearby to look after her. She never fully recovered from Dad's death.

EIGHT

The End of the
Fairy Tale

Jimmy and I attended a charity ball with our screenwriter friend, A.J. Carothers, and Caryl, his charming, beautiful wife. A.J. mentioned the difficulty they were having casting the role of Rosemary, the young, flirtatious roommate of Lesley Ann Warren in his new movie, "The Happiest Millionaire," a Disney musical. I sat across the table from him, trying to will him to see me for the role. He glanced at me from time to time with concern—he must have thought I had ants in my pants. A.J. only saw me as a friend, a young mother of two, not a 17-year-old flirtatious Rosemary.

Also at the table with us were Richard Sherman and his vivacious wife, Ursie. Richard had won an Oscar for composing the songs in "Mary Poppins." Later that evening, I was told that Richard had whispered to A.J., "Too bad Joyce isn't an actress—she'd be perfect for Rosemary." A.J. looked startled and said, "She *is* an actress!"

Richard and his brother, Robert, had composed the music for "The Happiest Millionaire." The next day I received a call from Ursie inviting Jimmy and me to dinner at their home.

After dinner, Richard said, "Joyce, I'd like to play you a song from 'The Happiest Millionaire,' the film that A.J. and I are working on. It's a song that Rosemary sings and I think you'd be perfect as Rosemary." I couldn't believe it. I grabbed Jimmy's hand and sat on the edge of the sofa, listening intently to "Bye-Yum Pum Pum," Rosemary's song.

I was asked to do a screen test with Leslie Ann Warren, and I got the part! Two weeks before shooting, I sneaked into Disney Studios to warm up at the ballet bar with the other dancers in the film. It was

important for me to get into dancing shape because I would be teaching Lesley Ann Warren the tango in the movie.

During my first official day at the studio, a huge bouquet of flowers arrived in my dressing room with a note from Walt Disney. "Although I know you've been sneaking onto the lot and working out with the

Dancing with Leslie Ann Warren

With Caryl and AJ Carothers, Richard and Ursie Sherman

dancers the last two weeks, I would like to welcome you on your first official day. Walt Disney."

A few days later, when I was on my way to the recording studio to do my song, Walt Disney came down from his office and said, "You're on your way to record, aren't you?"

"Yes. I'm trying not to be nervous, but I am."

He put his arm around me. "Let me walk you over there." I was so honored. I couldn't believe Walt Disney was escorting me. He gave me a wide smile. "I have big plans for you, young lady."

Sadly, Walt's plans for me never came to pass. "The Happiest Millionaire" was his last film.

*

Jimmy wasn't working and he was drinking again, a lot. In Hollywood and in all the fan magazines Jimmy and I were pictured as an ideal young couple with a perfect family, but it became harder and harder for me to keep up a happy front.

Sometimes in the evenings, Jimmy would invite friends over to our home to play a scary game, "The Hunters and the Hunted." During the game all the lights in the house were turned off. The hunters went into the kitchen with weapons, darts with rubber suction cups that shot out of plastic guns. The hunted hid in the living room. The light from the flames in the fireplace cast eerie shadows throughout the room. To me this game was too frightening. If you were shot, you were out of the game. It hurt to be shot, especially in the eye. A shot in the eye was called a "white flash." It was a sadistic game and I would beg not to play.

Other nights Jim stayed out late and came home drunk. He continued his game of creeping into the bedroom, crawling under the bed covers, and making a loud noise while he pulled on my foot, which scared me. If I cried, he yelled and called me names. While he yelled I tried to block out what he was saying by silently reciting the Lord's Prayer.

In the morning, the same routine: Jimmy would beg for forgiveness and I would forgive, always hoping things would change. I prayed that tomorrow would be a better day. A few days would go by, sometimes a week with no drinking, and then the drinking and abuse would start all over again.

The only way I could live with Jim was to start drinking myself. I never liked the feeling of being drunk. But in order to make love to him, which I thought was my wifely duty, I had to drink. He told me I was frigid and I believed him.

We both missed the theater, so Jimmy suggested we join an actor's workshop to keep our skills sharp. He had heard about a professional group of actors in the Valley who had a workshop over a bowling alley. They were doing a play for the public. I felt that this would also be a good outlet for Jimmy when he wasn't working; he could be working on scenes with other actors, not sitting around the house waiting for his agent to call.

The following week we went to see "Royal Hunt of the Sun." It was a nice theater with good actors. What a shock to see Roger Perry suddenly appear on stage! There went my heart again. I didn't hear a word of the play.

I had last seen Roger almost two years earlier on location in Las Vegas. I was certain that Jimmy wouldn't want to join this workshop because of Roger. Wrong! He thought the actors were terrific and it would be fun to practice with them. To make matters worse, I learned that Roger was now divorced. I mentioned this to Jimmy. He said, "I don't care."

We joined Theatre East, which had writers, directors and actors. There were some bit players and some well-known actors. At the workshop you could ask other actors if they wanted to do a scene with you and then decide who you would like to direct the scene. We rehearsed together and then performed for the members. After your scene, the group gave a helpful critique.

One night when Jim and I were having dinner with our friends Caryl and A.J. Carothers and Jack Weston, who was also a member of Theatre East, Jack said, "I have a great idea! I would like to direct you and Roger Perry in a scene from the musical 'On a Clear Day.' You really need to keep singing, Joyce. I think it would be a terrific idea.

Roger has a beautiful singing voice and you two would be really good together."

Be still my heart, was all I could think. Try to be casual. Try to be slightly interested. "That might be fun."

Jimmy said, "I think Jack is right. You should keep up your singing."

Jack said, "I'll talk to Roger to see if he wants to do it, OK?"

"Sure, if you want to."

It was one of the most difficult scenes for me to work on, not because of the play, but seeing Roger every day. He played a doctor who was trying to get me to see clearly. What I needed was to see more clearly in my real life! I have a picture taken during one of these rehearsals. In it I'm looking at Roger, he's looking at the drink in his hand, and I'm looking at him as if I could fall into his very being.

During rehearsals Roger was his usual kind self. I tried to hide my feelings. I told myself we were just two professionals working together. But there was more, an unexplained undercurrent, which I wasn't imagining—I could feel it.

Jimmy was working on scenes with other actors in the workshop. He was enjoying the work but it didn't stop his drinking. There were more late nights out.

One morning at breakfast, he grabbed the newspaper out of my hands. "I'm the man of the house, *I* see the paper first!" He threw a cereal box at my head. Mary, sitting in her highchair by the table, started to cry. I picked her up and went outside into the morning sunshine. My baby girl, how could I bring her up in a home where she would think this is the way to be treated by a man? I was also worried about Charlie, who was becoming very aggressive toward other children. He had to be watched while he played with others so that he didn't hurt them. Jimmy, often very aggressive towards Charlie and me, was a bad role model for Charlie. I realized I was a bad role model for Mary.

I desperately needed help. Church had always been a refuge for me as a child, and I needed to pray for help and guidance now more than ever. I had honored our marriage vows and now needed spiritual help to find out what to do.

I had always loved the beauty of the Episcopal Church, the sacredness of the service, and the acceptance of others and their beliefs. The service seemed to speak more about God's love than damnation. I thought I would like to be confirmed in the Episcopal faith and started taking confirmation classes at All Saints in Beverly Hills. It was comforting to go to those classes in the little chapel.

Jimmy made fun of me. One night he was angry because I wouldn't skip a class to go see a fight with him. I didn't care if I made him angry. I needed to find strength for my marriage, or at least for myself. I needed to find the right path for my children and for me, and to shake Roger out of my heart.

NINE

A Broadway Show and the Breaking Point

The phone rang, my agent asking me to audition for a Broadway play. Wow! That was exciting—a Broadway play, and the lead role! Maybe my prayers had been answered. If I got the role it would give me a break from Jimmy. I auditioned and went home to wait for a call. The call came a few days later, on my birthday.

"Hey, Joyce, it's Ron. You got it, kid! Warren Berlinger, the actor you read with, is playing opposite you."

"I can't believe it!" I was breathless. "Thank you, Ron." Oh, this would be just wonderful. The theater was my favorite; it's where I trained. I couldn't wait to tell Helen, Mother and Dad.

I called Jimmy into the kitchen and told him the good news. He was very excited for me. We began to make plans for the children during rehearsals. I told him I would take Mary with me because Mother would be happy to have her at the farm. I knew that Mrs. Buckley, the owner of Charlie's school, wouldn't let him miss school, so he would stay with Jimmy and the housekeeper. If the show became a hit, everyone could come to New York and we'd rent a house in Nyack near Helen. It all seemed a good plan to Jimmy. I dashed to the phone to call Helen.

"Hello, Mom, it's Joyce. I have the best news! I just got the lead in a Broadway play!"

There was a long pause on the other end of the phone.

"How dare you! How dare you go off and leave your husband and family!"

I felt as if someone had punched me in the stomach. I tried to pull myself together to explain our plan.

"I'm going to take Mary with me and Jimmy and Charlie will follow later." I said this very meekly, trying to recover from her rebuke. "How Dare You!" kept replaying in my head. Why had she reacted so strongly? This was what she had done all her life. Why didn't she want this life for me?

Recently I reread an old letter from Helen. She mentioned that late in life she had terrible guilt about going on the road and leaving her husband and son behind. Was she trying to save me from the guilt she once had?

The first day of rehearsals in New York City, I awoke early at the Algonquin Hotel, close to Times Square and Broadway. I had photos of Charlie, Mary, Jimmy, our dog, and our beautiful home on the walls. My stomach was too full of butterflies for breakfast. I wanted to go to Times Square before rehearsal and take it all in. I stood on the corner, my shiny new script tucked under my arm, and looked at the lights. Suddenly it hit me—I was going to be the lead in a Broadway play!

"Looking for a theater, little girl?"

I turned to see Jed Allen, one of the actors in the play, who was going to play my old boyfriend.

"I sure am."

"Let's go, then." Arm in arm, we headed to the theater.

On stage, the producer, director and cast sat around a table. I looked out into the dark theater at rows of empty seats. On opening night, these seats would be full of people dressed in evening clothes, their faces showing excitement about the new play.

Before the first reading of the play, there was a moment of silence. Everyone opened to the first page. This is always a time of magic, the first labor pain of a long and difficult birth. The first reading, late night rehearsals, changes in the script, notes from the director, and sadly, sometimes changes in the cast, all leading to opening night. The first reading of "The Paisley Convertible" was underway.

Weeks later, during the preview performances, the producer and director asked me to meet with them after the show. Of course I was very nervous. There comes a point in rehearsals and previews when an actor can be replaced. Was this the news I was going to get? Sam Waterston had replaced Warren Berlinger as my husband in the play. Now were they going to replace me? I hoped they were just going to give me notes about my performance.

The cast left the theater. The stage manager placed the work light on the empty stage and I walked down into the theater. I sat in the front row next to Jimmy Hammerstein, the director, and Mike Ellis, the producer. If they were going to replace me, I would be brave and strong, no tears. But the play seemed to be going well, and I was getting all the laughs I thought they wanted. Oh please, just tell me and get it over with!

Mike Ellis spoke first. "Joyce, you must promise me you will not tell a soul about what we need to do. It's very important for the play that you don't say anything to the cast, especially Sam. Can we count on you?"

I was puzzled. "Yes, of course."

"We are replacing Sam."

I couldn't believe it—he was such a good actor and wonderful to work with. He was so real, so grounded as a performer. "I don't understand. He's so good."

Jimmy Hammerstein said, "He just isn't getting the laughs we need. We want you to come in tomorrow morning and read with some actors. You must not say a word to anyone. We don't want Sam to know because he has to continue with the preview performances, and it would be upsetting to him. Do you understand?"

"I guess so."

Mike said, very sternly, "It would be too hard for Sam to carry on if he knew. Now, you must not tell him, understood!"

"Yes, I understand."

I was very upset. But I had always been taught that the director's word is God. You don't listen to anyone else, not the other actors, not your family, no one, just the director.

The next day, I read with several actors, including one I knew from television, Bill Bixby. They decided to cast Bill in the role because of his comedic abilities. Now I had to rehearse with Bill during the day and perform with Sam at night.

At the daytime rehearsals, the blocking was a bit different. It was difficult to switch gears. I loved working with Sam. Bill was a little slick, Sam more real. Bill had to get up to speed fast, so after performances at night, I would spend hours cueing him. I was exhausted.

One night after another late rehearsal, I walked into my hotel room, sat on the bed, and started to cry. It wasn't about the play; it was about going home to Jimmy. I looked at the pictures of Jimmy and our home. Slowly I stood up and turned each of the pictures around

"The Paisley Convertible" with Bill Bixby

so I didn't have to see them. I couldn't go back to him, and I couldn't stop crying.

Was I having a nervous breakdown? Jimmy always told me to go to the family doctor if I ever needed anything. I called Dr. John Marchand, the MacArthur family doctor. Dr. Marchand said he would pick me up early the next day for breakfast.

The next morning, I poured my heart out to him. He said, with no surprise in his voice, "I've been waiting for you to come to me for the last seven years. It's very unhealthy for you to be in this marriage to Jim. Don't you worry about your children? You said Jim's home with Charlie now. He could be drinking and smoking in bed and burn the house down. It's not safe for the children to live with him. Now, if you wish to be a martyr and stay in the marriage, that's up to you. But you have children and you have a responsibility to them."

I was shaken. My children, my children were in danger? Mary was safe with Mother while I was here, but Charlie? I became very alarmed. I told Dr. Marchand that we had a housekeeper who lived at home and was looking after Charlie. I tried to ease my mind, but he had really frightened me.

Dr. Marchand picked me up for lunch at the theater and again for dinner. We continued our talks. With concern, he said, "If you divorce Jim, you will be the Black Witch in Helen's eyes. You know that? She will make you the Black Witch. You have to be prepared for that."

"Helen told me not to marry Jimmy. She knows he has a drinking problem. I'm sure she'll understand."

"Don't forget her strong Catholic background and the fact that she stayed with Charlie through all his drinking and carrying on. She'll expect you to do the same. She may understand, but she will side with Jimmy."

"She told me I must never go to her if I had a problem with Jim. When she says bad things about Jimmy, I always stick up for him. I told her when she says bad things it hurts me, because I love him." Crying again, I said, "I don't know what to do."

"The pressures of the play have brought up the real pressure that you've been hiding. Joyce, just think about your children."

Books had taught me that being brought up in an unhappy home wasn't healthy for children. Tension and unhappiness had enveloped our home and squeezed my heart until I felt I couldn't breathe.

Jimmy flew in for opening night. It was important not to let the play down because of what I was going through. This wasn't the right time to talk to him about our marriage. I was still hoping to find a way to work everything out, and I didn't want Helen to be disappointed in me. If I could find a way to keep our marriage together, I would.

The opening seemed to go very well. The audience laughed a lot, and the director and producer were pleased. Afterward we went to Sardi's to wait for the reviews. When I walked into Sardi's, everyone broke into applause. I applauded too, until it hit me that this was the moment I had dreamed of—entering Sardi's after opening in a Broadway play and receiving acclaim! It was me they were applauding!

When the early reviews came out on television, ours were not very good. The papers that we waited for at Sardi's were better, but not good enough to keep the play running. My opening night flowers lasted longer than the run of the play. After our two-week run, I headed home with little Mary.

I talked to Jimmy about our marriage, the drinking and how it affected the children. I never mentioned my talks with Dr. Marchand. Jim was very understanding. He said he was going to stop drinking and everything would be all right again. I wanted so to believe him! But the drinking didn't stop.

I wasn't very strong. I was unsure and afraid. Jimmy frightened me. We continued going to the actors' workshop. When Jim was working on a scene he was less apt to drink a lot. That was a good thing.

Theatre East was going to do a public performance of a musical, "You Never Can Tell." The members always voted to see if a play merited a public performance. They didn't do many public performances, but they were excited to do this original musical based on the George Bernard Shaw play. Norman Cohen, Roger's good friend, adapted the play. Jim Ploss, another of his friends from college, wrote the lyrics, and Roger wrote the music. Roger was not only a wonderful actor with a beautiful singing voice, but a composer as well.

Roger was playing the romantic lead and Beverly Sanders was playing opposite him. I asked if I could do props for the play. Of course it was to be near Roger. I continued my confirmation classes at church, but they weren't doing much to turn my heart away from Roger.

As I stood in the wings watching rehearsals and listening to Beverly sing, I wished I had a beautiful voice like hers. But the Shaw play needed a certain acting style that Beverly was having difficulty mastering. After rehearsal, Norman caught up with me in the parking lot.

"Joyce, wait up. Have you got a minute?"

"Sure, what's up?"

"Jim Ploss, Roger, and I met with the director and we think we need to replace Beverly."

"Oh, no. That's going to be hard."

"I know, but she just doesn't have the style for that period. We wondered if you would audition for us."

"Oh, Norman, are you kidding? I would love to, but I can't sing like Beverly."

"Well, we'd like you to audition. Will you?"

I started to panic. Sing, all alone, with Roger and his two best friends watching me? I could do the style of the play all right, but I could never sing like Beverly.

"If you really think I could do it, I'll try."

I telephoned my good friend, Ray Henderson, my singing coach. Ray never wanted me to take proper singing lessons; he just wanted me to sing as much as possible. He felt the same way the staff at the American Academy had felt, that my voice was unique and if I took proper lessons, I would sound like everyone else.

Ray was a very close friend of Elsa Lanchester, known for her role as the bride in "The Bride of Frankenstein." He taught and composed music in the schoolroom at her home, a Frank Lloyd Wright in Hollywood. When I went there to practice with Ray, Elsa's Irish housekeeper would make me a hot cup of wonderful Irish tea. I often spent time talking in the kitchen with Elsa before my lessons. Sometimes Elsa would come into the schoolroom, listen to me sing, and give me helpful advice. Ray accompanied her when she did her nightclub acts, and occasionally, to my delight, she performed for me.

Now I stood in the schoolroom beside the piano, ready to sing for Norman, Jim and Ed Balin, the director. Thank heavens Roger didn't come to the audition. Why, I wondered? Was he afraid I would make a fool of myself? I certainly was afraid I would!

I don't think I sang very well; I was too nervous. When I finished, they applauded politely, then asked Ray if he would work with me on the songs. Did this mean they wanted me for the role?

Yes, it did! Now what was I to do? Playing opposite Roger in a romantic role—how to handle this? I hit the rail at church and prayed like crazy. I prayed not to give in to the feelings I had for Roger. Most of all I prayed that Jimmy and I could work things out. I felt I needed help from the minister. I took my marriage vows very seriously, and I knew Helen took my vows seriously.

I arranged for a meeting with the young minister and explained as much as I could about our marriage, without going into every detail. I didn't want him to have ill feelings about Jimmy. I told him about Jimmy's drinking and his behavior towards Charlie, which had become more severe. Charlie was only seven years old, and Jimmy spoke to him in a degrading way, putting him down with unkind words. I was concerned for my children, but because I respected my wedding vows, I didn't know what to do.

The minister suggested that I go to a marriage counselor. The counselor's office was small and messy, as he was. He reminded me of a used car salesman with slicked-back, greasy hair. I sat in a decrepit fake leather chair, with duct tape on the arms. I sat immobile in that big ugly chair, wanting to run out of the office. He was full of sexual innuendoes, the wrong therapist for me. I never went back again.

I was becoming desperate for help. Jimmy was staying out again until early morning. He was always angry and upset. Being in Roger's arms in love scenes during rehearsals didn't help one bit. I told Jimmy I thought we should separate. Our lives had come apart at the seams, and perhaps if we had time apart we could find our way back to each other. If not, we could go on with our lives and not hurt our children by keeping them in a tense house without love.

Jim and I held hands in the attorney's office in Beverly Hills. We said we needed to have a separation agreement and hoped that after a while we might be able to work things out. The attorney was a nice man who seemed to care about us. I didn't know how or what to feel. I just couldn't stay with Jimmy any longer. Of course now he was being loving and kind and said he wanted to work things out, the same old tune to the same old song. It reminded me of a song Dale Evans wrote and sang to me once:

> Your roses say you're sorry, but I've heard it so many times.
> Baby, I know music and I know all your rhymes.
> How many times must I forgive you?
> I can't live without you and I can't live with you.
> Baby, I'll take you back with your roses, one more time.

This time I was going to follow through. I wouldn't be a martyr and I wouldn't bring my children up in a home without love.

A few days after our meeting, the attorney telephoned me. In a very apologetic voice he said, "Joyce, I'm sorry, but I won't be able to handle you and Jim. He wants me to do unscrupulous things. I'm sorry, but I wish not to be involved with your case. I suggest you get your own attorney."

I was dumbfounded. What was he talking about? When I got off the phone I told Jimmy about our conversation. Jimmy said he was going to go with Dick Schmidt's attorney. Dick and his wife Yvonne, friends of ours, were in the process of getting divorced, and Jimmy, without telling me, had decided to seek his own counsel.

I called an old friend of my family, Don Moss, and asked for his advice. Don sent me to someone in downtown Los Angeles. When I saw the attorney, I told him I hoped Jimmy and I might get back together after the separation. I told him about the drinking and late nights. Still wanting to protect Jimmy, I didn't tell him about the affairs.

At breakfast, Jim looked at me and said, quite casually, "My attorney said that it would look better for me if you and the children moved out."

I was shocked.

It wasn't until later that I found out this was a way for Jim to discredit me by saying I had abandoned him. That made me even more resolute to get away from Jimmy as fast as I could. He was asking his wife and children to leave their home and go to a cheap rental. I didn't care. I needed to get out.

The night before our moving day, Jimmy had been drinking and pointed a gun at my head. I was terrified of him and frightened for the children. I couldn't move out fast enough. I didn't want to fight. It was agony breathing the same air he did. His meanness had destroyed my forgiveness for him.

We had built a nursery and bath for Mary when she was born, and also a swimming pool. It was the end of August and very hot. The children were enjoying the pool. Now I was going to move them to a little rented house I had found, with no air conditioning and no swimming pool. But it was going to be filled with peace and love. In the morning I had to explain to Charlie why we were leaving his daddy and our home. How do you explain this to a child? I sat close to Charlie and held his hand.

"It's like having a good friend who likes to go fishing with you. Then one day, your friend says he doesn't want to fish anymore. He says he would rather play baseball, but you don't like baseball. So you go fishing and he plays baseball and you don't see each other as much. That's what it's like with Daddy and me." Charlie looked at me as if he understood. He didn't seem sad and he didn't cry. All I could think was, what a dopey explanation for something that would change the course of the children's lives and mine forever.

✳

The gardener came and loaded our few possessions into the back of his truck. The children's bedroom furniture, their paintings and toys, a table and four chairs from the kitchen, a bed for Katherine, the house-keeper, and a twin bed from the guest room for me.

Katherine would stay with us to help with the children while I was working. She would go with the children every other weekend while they visited Jim. I wanted her to be watchful every minute for their safety.

With Mary in my arms, I took one last look at our first family home, a home that had often seen joyful times. But the fearful times had cast an ugly shadow over the entire house and turned it into a dark and evil place.

Jimmy stood at the door as I walked by with Mary. I hoped he would say how sorry he was to cast his children out of their home and hoped that we might be able to work things out. Sneering, he said, "You'll be back. You can't live without a swimming pool and a maid."

I kept walking.

Charlie climbed in the front seat of the truck next to the gardener, and I climbed in next to him. Mary, not quite two, sat on my lap. We pulled out of the long driveway lined with blue jacaranda blossoms and watched our beautiful English carriage home grow smaller and smaller as we traveled down the lane. When the truck reached the highway, all I could think was "Born Free, as Free as the Wind Blows."

Katherine and I had the little house shipshape in no time. Our rather dilapidated fridge was filled with food. The children's pictures were hung in their rooms and their toys were arranged. I put a bouquet

of flowers on the kitchen table and turned up the music on the radio. At the last moment, I had loaded my wicker rocking chair in the truck. I sat down and picked Mary up and held her in my lap. In peace, we rocked back and forth and watched Charlie play.

Together wherever we go

(125)

TEN

Be Still, My Heart

That night I went to the theater. We were still performing "You Never Can Tell." After the show I asked Roger if he would walk with me to my car. When we reached the car, I turned to him.

"Roger, I left Jimmy. The children and I have moved to a rented house."

There was a long silent moment. Roger looked at me and said, for the very first time, "I love you."

I invited Roger to come to dinner. Our rented house was painted a sick yellow on the outside and a gray ghost color inside. The yard was filled with weeds, but my heart was filled with joy as I prepared dinner for Charlie, Mary and Roger. After dinner, with the children all tucked into bed, Roger and I threw two big sofa pillows on the floor in front of the television and watched "The Umbrellas of Cherbourg," a romantic French film whose title song had the lyrics, "If it takes forever, I will wait for you."

✳

A few weeks later, Roger asked me to go away to Laguna for the weekend. I knew what that meant—a tornado of butterflies attacked my stomach. I had only been with one man in my whole life, and as much as I desperately wanted to be with Roger, I was frightened-nervous-anxious-excited-longing... Jimmy had told me I was frigid. Was I?

I asked Katherine if she could stay overnight with the children for two nights as I was going to visit a friend. I held my breath for her answer. If she said no, that meant I wasn't supposed to go.

"Sure, no problem."

I explained to Jimmy that it would be a good idea for Katherine to be with the children when they went to stay with him. It was important for them to have as much continuity in their life as possible. What I didn't say was how concerned I was because of his drinking.

Roger and me in "You Never Can Tell"

The last night of the performance of "You Never Can Tell," the night Roger and I were going away, was a bit of a blur. My bag was backstage and I could think of nothing but what would happen later that night with Roger.

My heart was pounding as Roger opened the car door for me. Seated at the wheel, Roger reached over and patted my hand. He looked so handsome and gave me the kindest reassuring smile. Oh, those blue eyes!

At the motel, Roger put our suitcases down and I sat on the edge of the bed facing the window.

"They have hot chocolate. Would you like some?"

"Oh yes, thank you."

I smiled nervously. Hoping to have enough time while he went for the chocolate, I slipped into the bathroom, brushed my teeth, changed into my new nightie and sprayed on my perfume, L'Air du Temps.

While still in the bathroom, I heard Roger come in. I took a deep breath and opened the bathroom door. Trying to look cool as I stood there, hoping he couldn't see my knees shaking under my demure nightie, I smiled at him. Was he disappointed that instead of a sexy siren, it was just me—shy, frightened me?

"Come sit down, here's hot chocolate for you." He patted the side of the bed next to where he was sitting. We sat side by side like flies on the sugar bowl, drinking our hot chocolate. Shy smiles passed back and forth.

"Well, I'll go get ready for bed."

The minute he went into the bathroom I jumped under the covers and faced away from the bathroom. I don't think I took a breath until I heard him come out of the bathroom. He turned the lights off and climbed in next to me.

"Are you scared?"

"Uh-huh."

"Me too. I love you."

"I love you."

With those wonderful words, I learned that night what love really was—the tender, caring touch of someone who can change your whole world and make you feel truly loved. That night, years of longing turned into something that can only be experienced with a deep and meaningful connection between two people. All through the night we made love over and over again.

In the morning we walked hand in hand to the beach, as if we were in a magic bubble. We passed people on the street and on the beach and swimmers splashing in the ocean. But they were outside. In our bubble you could not hear a sound, only the quiet knowledge that this was our world, serene and full of awe.

This was love.

The happiest of days followed. Roger arranged camping trips for us and our children. Roger's children Chris and Dana, eight and three, were each a year older than Charlie and Mary. What fun we had, building camp fires, pitching tents! They were the old army-type tents, with stakes you drive into the ground and secure with rope. The little ones slept in a trailer hitched to the back of the car. We were not far from Los Angeles in Big Bear, a little mountain town.

Roger and I had our sleeping bags close together. We held hands and looked up at the stars. As we drifted off to sleep, the smell of pine trees filled the air.

On a weekend when Jimmy had the children, Roger thought it would be fun for the two of us to drive up the coast to Big Sur. He arranged our trip, including an overnight in a log cabin nestled in a forest. Roger and I hadn't had any romantic alone time together since our trip to the beach. Because of the children, I wouldn't think of having a man sleep over, even in the era of "free love" and people living together without being married… not this mother! So I was really looking forward to our trip up the coast.

On the drive from L.A. to Santa Barbara, Roger noticed a brown car that seemed to be following us. We stopped in a little café overlooking the ocean and had a cup of coffee. When we came out and continued on the road, the car Roger thought was following us had pulled over to the side of the road with the hood up. The minute we drove by, he slammed down the hood of the car and started to follow us again. Roger said it might be Jimmy trying to prove I was having an affair. I was, but I thought it was all right since we were separated and getting divorced, and Jimmy had had affairs. Roger was afraid that Jim might try to take the children away from me, if he knew we were seeing each other. That really frightened me. We stopped someplace so that I could call my good friend, Barbara Login. I asked her if she would do me a great favor.

"Could you please meet me in Santa Barbara?" I explained the situation. "We need to meet in a very public place, the El Paseo restaurant, OK? If you would like, we can go up to Big Sur for a couple of nights."

She said she'd love to go. This way, the person following us would think that I was just meeting a girlfriend and going away with her for the night.

Poor Roger, what a good sport and caring guy to have arranged a romantic weekend, only to be replaced by my girlfriend. Barb met us with hugs and greetings, a big show for whoever was following us. Barb and I headed to Big Sur and Roger headed back to LA.

So long, romantic weekend.

*

As the divorce proceeding drew near, I wanted to make certain the sordid facts of our marriage were not made public. Most of all, I didn't want Helen to know about the way Jimmy had behaved, the cruel way he treated me and the children when he was drinking. I didn't want to hurt her more than I already had by divorcing her son, an act that created a deep tear in the fabric of our loving relationship. I wondered if it could ever be mended.

My attorney told me reporters were asking questions about the divorce. I asked him please not to say anything; I never really told him everything about Jimmy. Just like in school, I was always trying to protect Jimmy. Why?

One day, returning from the market and fishing for the house keys, I dropped some apples, which rolled under the back of the car. When I stooped down to pick up an apple, I noticed, attached to the underside of the car, a black box with two wires sticking out of it. I thought for a moment that Jimmy had placed a bomb under the car! Terrified, I dropped the grocery bag and grabbed little Mary out of her car seat. I went inside with Mary in my arms, put her down, and rushed to the telephone to call the police. They came to look at the car and told me it was a tailing device so that I could be followed. Thank heavens, it wasn't a bomb! But what a terrible, sinking feeling to realize Jimmy was having me followed.

One night after going to a Theatre East workshop, I walked to my car with Roger and under the dashboard I saw wires and strips of tape. Roger said it looked as if someone had put some sort of device in my car to hear or do something. I felt more violated than frightened. Jimmy was so desperate—but why? What did he hope to prove?

At the time of our divorce, there was no such thing as "no-fault divorce." You had to prove a reason. Maybe he was afraid that I would bring up all his drinking and abuse, and he was trying to find things I had done wrong. Years later, Jimmy told me that the night I found all the tape hanging in my car, he was on the hill across from where my car was parked and had a gun aimed at me and Roger. He said, "You know, I could have a contract taken out on you. I know people."

I never said anything to anyone but Roger. I should have told my attorney. I should have asked for help. I was afraid but didn't want Helen to know how bad the situation was. She wrote, "Since you are shedding my son as your husband, I can no longer sign as Mom. I guess it will just have to be Grammy (as the children called her). I will naturally have to go with my son."

I remembered her words to me. "If you have problems in your marriage, don't come to me." I didn't. I had to be able to give the court a reason for the divorce. I asked Barb if she could be a witness to Jim's bad behavior. I said, "Let's just think of the least disturbing thing you can say."

She had seen Jim throw a glass of vodka at me, and she had also seen him throw a cereal box at me at the breakfast table. We decided to go with the cereal box. Right before we went into the courtroom, Jim and I met to sign the settlement papers. I received only half of what our home was worth when we originally purchased it five years earlier, before adding an additional bedroom and bath and swimming pool. I asked for support, a very small amount, for Charlie and Mary's medical and school expenses. I asked for no alimony. I took some of the furniture, which I had purchased with my earnings. He kept my jewelry, our wedding gifts, a beautiful dining table, and two leather chairs we had purchased in Spain. In exchange, I asked for one item that was important to me, a lovely English hutch. I took none of the artwork, which Helen had given to us, nor did I ask for the money she had given to each of us, separately, every year. I wanted out with as little fuss as possible. It wasn't wise, but I was too afraid to fight or argue.

Outside the courtroom, the two of us sat alone. Jim put the document in front of me and said, "If you don't sign this, you're not going to get this back." He held up my Dad's gold watch that he had left in his will to Charlie. Biting my lips and holding back tears that I had held in check for so long, I looked at the person I had dated in school, loved for so long, had two children with. All I felt was loathing and a great sense of pity.

ELEVEN

Moving On

I found a cute ranch house in Sherman Oaks, with rooms for Charlie and Mary and a bathroom for them to share. The previous owners had added a maid's room, good for Katherine, and there was a bedroom and bath for me. A fenced-in swimming pool took up most of the backyard. It was certainly smaller than our home with Jimmy, but it would be a happy home.

Mother very kindly shipped some furniture that she had in storage from the farm. It helped furnish our home with happy memories and comfort. There was Dad's antique wooden desk, where I used to watch him pay bills and write letters. Now I sat there with Roger by my side, creating a budget. For my bedroom, Mother gave me the maple canopied bed she and Dad had shared at the farm.

I choose striking wallpaper for the entry hall. My upright piano sat to the right of the fireplace. It was here that Roger wrote the musical "Make a Promise, Keep a Promise." It was also where my friend

Richard Sherman, the composer, played music from "Chitty Chitty, Bang Bang."

Roger and his old friend, Norman Cohen, pulled weeds and bushes out of the front yard. They seemed pleased with their pay of lemonade and cookies and spaghetti for dinner. I had the house painted white with black shutters and a red front door with a brass doorknocker. We planted birch trees beneath Charlie's window, and I thought a maple tree would put the finishing touch in the front yard. One fall day Roger and I planted a maple tree about five feet tall. We stood back and surveyed our work. Not bad.

✳

My agent called and asked me to audition for a new show, "The Brady Brunch."

I was offered the role, just what I needed! Many actors came to do screen tests with me. Among the men who tried out as my husband, Robert Reed got the part. Then children auditioned to be my three little girls. Three who looked a lot like me were chosen. The housekeeper would play the straight role, and I was to provide the humor.

Sherwood Schwartz, the producer, had already had a hit with "Gilligan's Island." I was asked to lose five pounds, as my round face looked even rounder on TV. I went to Louise Long, who was known to take pounds off actors just before they started shooting a new show. Torture Chamber, it was! She would lie you down on a massage table and beat you black and blue. Then she would put little electric things on your fat parts and you would lie there being semi-electrocuted! To add insult to lots of injury, you were given a diet of eggs and tomatoes to eat... nothing else!

Every morning for a week, a limo arrived to pick me up. I staggered out and climbed into the back seat, weak from lack of food and sleep. The constant growling of my stomach kept me awake all night. The costume designer and I went to the finest stores in Beverly Hills, searching for just the right outfits for the show. In the afternoons I staggered back to be beaten black and blue once again. When the week ended, I had indeed lost five whole pounds.

Two days before we were to start shooting, the director and producer came to the wardrobe department to see me dressed in various outfits and select the ones they liked best. I twirled into the room in a beautiful yellow dress.

With a big smile I said, "This is for the garden wedding scene. What do you think? It's pretty, isn't it?"

"Yes, it's quite nice." Said without enthusiasm. Perhaps they would prefer another dress. Next I showed them a lovely blue suit.

"This is for the going away outfit after the wedding. Do you like it?"

"Sure." I looked at the two men, their faces downcast.

"Is something wrong?"

"Joyce, sit down, honey." Sherwood patted the seat next to him. "We have a problem."

"What's wrong?"

"Marty Starger, head of ABC in New York, wants Florence Henderson for your role. She just finished a film and became available. We're doing everything we can to change his mind. We feel that if you do the show, it will be more like 'The Lucy Show' and if Florence does it, it'll be more like 'The Donna Reed Show.' We're fighting for you, but New York has the final say. I am so sorry."

"That's OK." I was trying to make them feel better; they looked so sad.

"Marty saw film of the two of you, and he just thinks you're too young looking."

To make things more complicated, Florence and I had the same agent, who didn't have an incentive to fight for me. Sherwood wasn't able to change Marty's mind, so they had to recast the housekeeper to make her the funny one and Florence the straight one. Of course "The Brady Bunch" became a huge success.

I was given the blue going-away suit for my troubles—very appropriate. Sherwood, the dear man, promised I would be in his next show.

On some nights when the children were asleep, Roger would park several blocks from the house, climb over our back fence and quietly come through the French doors into my bedroom. Oh happy me, being loved by such a caring and gentle man. Roger would be gone before the sun, before the children woke up.

Once after I traveled to visit my mother, I found on my bed two gifts and a red rose. The first gift was a pair of bedroom slippers in a nice box. The second present was more meaningful. I had mentioned one day that I wanted to have a prayer book, and when I unwrapped the second package, there was a white prayer book. I have had that prayer book by my bed to this very day.

Roger did many thoughtful things for me. One day when he came to visit, I was very sick with a fever, and he wrapped me in a blanket and took me to his doctor. No one ever cared for me the way Roger did. But there came a time that I questioned Roger's love for me. I had been offered the lead in a Broadway play, every actor's dream. When I was negotiating the salary and talking about it with Roger, he said I needed to be paid enough so that he would be able to go with me to New York. I said I might lose the job if I ask for too much money. He said I had to try.

They wouldn't give me any more than what they had offered. Roger said it was up to me. I turned it down. I wanted so to do the play, but I didn't want to lose Roger. It was the first time I felt disappointed in him. I wanted him to be happy for me and supportive. I felt he was only thinking of himself, but I rationalized his reaction, telling myself that he loved me so much he couldn't be without me. I felt needed and gave up my dream.

Later in our relationship, when other things started to unravel, I looked back on giving up the play and realized that I resented Roger for not encouraging me to go to New York.

— TWELVE —

Shattered Dreams

New Year's Eve was coming, and the children would be with Jimmy for the week. Roger asked me if I would like to go to a cabin in Big Bear with a group of friends from Theatre East. He said that everyone chips in and rents a cabin. They bring casseroles and food for the week. I thought it sounded like great fun and it was! The earth was covered with snow and the branches of the pine trees that we had camped under in the fall had exchanged their green dress to a lovely white. The week was filled with talk and laughter, good food and friends. During the day we walked in the snow and took turns sliding down a hill on an inner tube. When we got too cold we retreated to the cabin and warmed our cold hands in front of the cozy fireplace. I was so happy.

Helen was coming to town and I wanted so to see her. I loved her very much and knew how unhappy she was about our divorce. From time to time I'd send her pictures of the children with a note. The children and I invited her to come for tea on Valentine's Day. She agreed.

We made Valentine's cookies to go with the tea, and the children made Valentine's cards to give her. I was nervous when she arrived, but she greeted the children with open arms and gave me a rather stiff hug. That's OK, I thought. She's here. We sat around the coffee table in the living room and the children chatted on and on as I served cookies and tea. She looked around the living room and said, "It's interesting how the furniture fits into this tiny house." I was a bit taken back. A few days after her visit, I received a very nice note from her saying that she had found the children more engaging then ever and she could put aside her old-fashioned notions and be happy that Jimmy and I were both doing well.

Roger and I shared many wonderful times together, sometimes with the children and sometimes we had the house to ourselves. I never noticed that Roger drank a lot. I never saw him drunk. Of course I must have, but I was blind to it. He wasn't abusive like Jimmy, not at all. But one day he was angry and threw a pillow at Charlie. I don't remember why. But it was disturbing and something was familiar about the tone, the behavior. I was concerned—I didn't like it or the feeling I had.

A few days later Roger said he would like to move in with me, maybe even have a baby, but not get married. Even though other people were living openly together by then, this really shook me. He knew how I felt.

I was working a lot during that time in TV shows, while Roger's work was at a standstill. The thought occurred to me that he might want to live off me.

A month or so later we were both cast in a play together, playing husband and wife. A friend from Theatre East workshop, Ed Mallory, was directing. The play was successful and we were asked to go to Philadelphia with it.

While in Philly, Roger and I stayed with my mother in her small, ever-so-proper Rittenhouse Square apartment. I slept with mother and Roger slept on the sofa in the living room. During this time Roger had become withdrawn, and one day Mother commented on his manners. My mother was over the top when it came to proper manners. She said in her most snobby voice, "Are you certain you could sit across the table from someone with manners like that every day of your life?" I often felt Mother put too much emphasis on manners rather than on character.

During rehearsals, Ed spent a lot of time rehearsing my scenes with Mariette Hartley. He was a good director. I admired him for his talent and without realizing it, I had developed feelings for him. He was a Southern gentleman with savoir faire.

Roger took me to New York City when we closed in Philly. He had chosen an affordable hotel, The Edison. It was not what I was used to. Our room was very plain. The double bed had a faded bedspread that changed colors when the neon light outside the window flashed

"The Happiness Bench" with Tom Bellin, Roger, me,
Mariette Hartley, John Aniston and Ed Mallory

on and off. Suddenly I felt that Roger wasn't the right person for me. I thought maybe he didn't care about esthetics and the niceties of life. Mother's snobbish remark came back to me (I'm upset at myself when I feel snobby about something that I've been taught isn't proper. I don't like being judgmental; it's not a good trait). I had a stomach ache that night and didn't want to make love. Roger was upset. I know none of this would have mattered to me if I'd been feeling good about him.

The happy-go-lucky, loving mood of our relationship started shifting. I knew I had lost some respect for Roger ever since he asked to move in. He was offended that Ed paid more attention to my scenes with Mariette Hartley than to his scenes. He became angry, moody and not fun to be with.

After the play closed and we were back home, Roger took me out to dinner at a Mexican restaurant to celebrate my birthday. During dinner I asked Roger what he wanted to do with his life. How was he going to earn a living when he wasn't acting? What did our relationship mean? I was pushing, probing, and badgering him. He was very quiet.

On the way home after dinner, we didn't speak. At the driveway to my house, instead of coming around to open the car door for me, he reached across the front seat, opened my side of the car door and said, "Goodbye, forever!"

Stunned, I got out of the car. But if this was what he wanted and why he had been acting so distant and mean… so be it! I went into my bathroom and took down the framed picture over the tub—an old fashioned lady going through the different stages of her life: engagement, trousseau, wedding, honeymoon, new love, a baby. With tears rolling down my face, I smashed it in the bathtub. The frame broke in two and the glass shattered all over, just as my dreams with Roger had shattered.

THIRTEEN

The Eyes of Love

It was nine days before Christmas, time to shake off the sadness that was covering me like an old wet coat and get on with my life. I had so many blessings, two beautiful children, a lovely home, and I was lucky to be working. I refused to give in to sadness. I reminded myself it was up to me to create my own happiness.

Out came the Christmas decorations, green garlands, Christmas candles, red Christmas balls and wreaths with red bows. With everything in place, it was time for a Christmas Eve tree-trimming party! I certainly wasn't going to let the children see my sadness, and all the activity helped. Of course, the friends I invited were also friends of Roger's. It was hard to see them and not be with Roger.

The children were all snug in their beds when the guests started arriving and helping themselves to eggnog. The living room was filled with holiday chatter. The guests started to decorate our tree, and soon it sparkled with lights and ornaments.

The word had spread about Roger and me not being together. Thankfully, only Norman, Roger's good friend and now mine, took me aside to say that he was sure things would work out. I smiled and let myself feel a moment of sadness, but not for long. There were guests to look after, it was Christmas Eve and I had two little children who needed me.

Arriving late with a large, beautifully wrapped gift was Ed Mallory. He looked dapper in suit and tie. He was tall, with blue eyes and curly dark blonde hair. Ed was graceful, witty and self-assured. He cut a commanding, romantic figure near the fireplace. What a nice person, I thought. Recently divorced from his second wife, he was renting a Spanish-style home in Hollywood. It was nice to see him and so thoughtful that he brought a gift. Little did I know that this would be Hollywood husband number two.

Ed lingered after all the other guests left and asked me to open his gift, a lovely set of crystal glasses. He asked me how I felt about the break-up with Roger. I told him how sad I was and he talked about his divorce from Pam. We talked for a long time until I said I must say goodnight as I had gifts to put out for the children from Santa Claus. He asked if he might help. It was fun playing Santa together, and I saw another side of Ed, whom I had heard had such a temper that he had once smashed his fist through a wall at Theatre East over a creative dispute.

Norman had moved into to Ed's house after Ed was divorced and told me he was very lonely. Oh dear, Joyce to the rescue. I invited Norman and Ed to dinner a few times and Ed asked me if I would go out with him. A date?

I really didn't feel up to anything romantic. "Sure, if it's just friendship."

Ed made dinner for the children and me several times at his home. Often he invited us to go swimming there. It was fun, and my heart was healing a bit.

Ed suggested that I might enjoy going to see him on the set of "Days of Our Lives," in which he played Dr. Bill Horton and had become a matinee idol. After work we could go to dinner.

When Ed finished work, he asked if I would like to go over to the set of "Laugh In," a very popular NBC show. I hesitated at first. Roger had mentioned numerous times a friend of his on that show, JoAnne Worley. Once he had asked me why I couldn't be more like her. I thought it would be fun to watch them shoot, and I was curious about JoAnne.

Of all days, Roger was there, on the floor near where they were filming. Ed and I were sitting up higher, out of sight from Roger. When I saw Roger, a flood of emotions bombarded my heart. I wanted to run away, I froze in my seat, I couldn't move. I averted my eyes, thinking if I didn't look at him, the pain would go away. When I dared to glance his way again, Roger had left the sound stage and I was able to breathe again. I told Ed I was hungry and we left. I didn't get to see JoAnne.

New Year's Eve was approaching and Ed asked if I would like to go to a party with him. I agreed. At the party I should have seen a red flag, but it was New Year's Eve and excessive drinking wasn't unusual. Ed certainly drank, but he didn't become mean, just sleepy. I drove myself home. The next day Ed called to apologize. I said I understood and not to worry.

Ed and I were seeing each other more often, quite casually at first. When my friend, Barbara, and her boyfriend were going skiing at Mammoth, she asked if Ed and I would like to go along. Oh dear, did this mean sleeping together? I really wasn't ready for this, but I knew Ed was. I thought I might be falling in love with him. But was I? We went skiing, shared a bed and made love, but it wasn't the same feeling I had had with Roger. I worried that now I'd gone to bed with three different men. What was I, some kind of tramp? I'd always wanted to be with one man, and since it wasn't Jimmy or Roger, did this mean it was going to be Ed?

I grappled with whether he was the right person for the children and me. I was full of questions, but I wanted so much to be married and have a home. I thought it would be best for the children. They would feel secure, having a home and a gentle man in their life. Ed was very sensitive, kind and romantic.

One night Ed and I went to the Beverly Hilton for dinner. There was candlelight and a violinist, all very romantic. After we went dancing, Ed parked his car on top of Mulholland Drive, overlooking the lights of the San Fernando Valley. We listened to the radio and talked. The song "You're Just Too Good to Be True" was playing. Ed said that was how he felt about me and how much he loved me. Would I marry him?

For a moment I just looked at him and smiled. I didn't answer, just leaned over and gave him a tender kiss. I don't know what he thought. He started the car and we drove down the hill into the valley without saying a word. When we reached Van Nuys Boulevard, Ed asked if I'd like to stop for a glazed donut, my favorite. While I was eating the donut, I looked at him and gave him my answer—"Yes."

*

Ed and I needed to find a home. While he was at work I searched up and down the valley. It was best to stay in the valley, since Ed's work was there and I wanted the children to go to school as far from Beverly

Hills as possible. I thought the valley was a more stable family environment without the pretensions of Beverly Hills.

In Granada Hills I found a ranch house with a red barn, a guesthouse and a creek that ran through the property at the bottom of a hill. It could have been a farm in the middle of Iowa. The guesthouse would be for a live-in housekeeper, which we needed because I was working a lot. Perfect! Ed loved it and so did the children. At the time Ed didn't have the finances to share in the purchase, so I paid for it and put it in both our names. We decided to give the farm a name. Mother and Dad had named their farm, and I thought that was nice. Ed agreed. We both liked Shakespeare's sonnets and read them to each other, so Sonnet Hill Farm was the name we chose. Our friends got together to have an engagement party for us at Ed's home. Joan Fuhrman, another friend of Roger's who had remained my friend, came up with the idea for the party, "Help Make Sonnet Hill a Farm." Well, they sure did. Our gifts were chickens, ducks, and a donkey!

The wedding was to be at the farm, outdoors at sunset. The children would be in the wedding ceremony, along with my good friend, Barbara, as my Maid of Honor. Carol Montgomery, Ed's sister, would be my Matron of Honor. Mary was the flower girl and Charlie, age nine, and Doug, Ed's nephew, age eight, were young ushers. They looked so cute in their navy blazers with a daisy stuck in their buttonholes.

Chairs were lined up outside the red barn, facing the canyon below. An arch of flowers stood over the minister. Baskets of flowers on stands surrounded us, and garlands of flowers hung on the barn. After the wedding we had a receiving line while hors d'oeuvres and champagne were served.

I asked Barbara and Carol to wear old-fashioned milkmaid dresses, and I had little milkmaid caps made for them. Barbara, my very sophisticated artist friend, wasn't happy, but she went along with it. I wore an old-fashioned long calico dress printed with little pink roses and a bonnet copied after one that my dear friend, Lillian Gish, had worn in a movie. I carried a bouquet of pink tea roses.

Wedding day with Ed, Wes Kenney, Susan Seaforth and Susan Flannery

It was a real country wedding.

Just before the wedding I had a moment to be alone with my thoughts. Lately Ed hadn't been able to make love. I had suggested we see a counselor before going ahead with the marriage. Something just didn't feel right. Maybe he didn't love me? He convinced me that he did love me and everything would be fine. It was just wedding jitters, he said. I wanted to believe him.

When the guests were seated and the piano music began, I took the arm of Don Moss, a friend of Mother and Dad's, who gave me away. We started down the aisle. Was I doing the right thing? I smiled as I walked down the aisle to a song from Finian's Rainbow, "Follow the Man Who Follows his Dream."

Ed didn't want to invite Roger to the wedding. As I walked down the aisle, from somewhere deep in my heart, I hoped Roger would come running in, yelling, "No! No! Stop! She loves me and I love her."

Barbara used to ask her boyfriend, "Why don't you look at me the way Ed looks at Joyce, with so much love in his eyes?" Barbara later told me that the minute I said, "I do," she never saw that look again from Ed.

FOURTEEN

Like Sands Through the Hourglass

Helen, who had just celebrated her seventieth birthday, came to visit at the farm. She had been given a lavish party in Hollywood, arranged by Carol Burnett. The magnificent birthday cake, covered with tiny pink roses all over the top, was a work of art. All the guests had been given cupcake versions of the larger cake. Helen brought the giant cake with her to share with the children. I made a pot of English tea and placed china cups, dishes and milk on a tray. Helen asked me to serve the cake. I cut a slice for each of the children and one for Helen and me. While eating the cake, I suddenly got an idea. "Okay, everyone, that's enough, we don't want to spoil our dinners." I whisked the cake to the kitchen as fast as I could, before I heard cries for more. It had dawned on me that this would be the perfect cake for Norman and Dolores' engagement party next month. All I had to do was cover it carefully with tin foil and freeze it.

A month later, the engagement party was in full swing, and it was now time for dessert, the pièce de résistance: Helen's birthday cake, now an engagement cake! I had artfully filled the space where cake was missing with a small silver vase filled with fresh flowers that matched the little roses of icing on top of the cake. It looked great! No one would know. Pleased with my accomplishment, I placed it in front of Norman and Dolores, while the guests gathered to watch them cut the cake. There were "ooohs" and "aaahs." Mary's little hands were on the edge of the table by the cake. She stood wide-eyed, waiting for a piece. Dolores looked at her and said, "Mary, darling, you get the very first piece." Mary looked up and said, "But I already had a piece of Grammy's birthday cake."

We had lots of parties at the farm. Ed really got into decorating for a party. Barbara and Ian's wedding reception was held in our Red Barn. Tables were set around the swimming pool in front of the barn and Ed had cleverly hung the brass chandelier from our bedroom in a tree by the pool. We put yellow tablecloths and blue napkins on the tables, and I arranged centerpieces of blue Lily of the Nile and daisies. It did look lovely. Ed had written a toast to the newlyweds. After dinner and wedding cake, Ed stood to make his toast. All heads turned towards him and watched as he slowly slid under the table, drunk.

As much fun as it was planning our parties, they usually ended with Ed very drunk. He was never mean when he drank, but he became loud. He would shout Shakespeare to me until all hours. I was worried he would frighten the children. He seemed to be so troubled, often demeaning himself.

Carol Ann, Ed's sister, had moved down the street from us. We had the best time baking together and watching her children, Doug and Jolie, swim and play with Charlie and Mary. The girls took ballet class together and on occasion Carol Ann and I would pack up the kids and head for Yosemite or other fun road trips. She wasn't happily married, and I was getting more concerned about my marriage. But I had what I had always hoped for, a close family.

Carol Ann asked if I would look after the children while she and Lee, her husband, went to China on a business trip. She was working hard to keep her marriage together and I wanted to help. Hoping that a trip together without the children might bring them closer, I said the children could stay with us.

One fall day, I went outside to get the morning paper. Ed had gone to work and the children were all at school. The smell of autumn was in the air, leaves being burned, reminding me of autumn back home in Pennsylvania. Over my morning cup of tea I remembered autumn at the farm, warm memories of times with Mother and Dad. In the fall we would sit on the terrace with our coffee, admiring the wondrous job God had done painting the trees with beautiful colors.

Later that afternoon, with the children home from school and having milk and cookies, I noticed an orange glow outside the window. I went out and saw the sky had turned an ominous shade of orange, and there was a strong burning smell.

People don't burn their leaves in California! I rushed inside and turned on the television. A news reporter said, "A fire that started this morning in Newhall has joined with another major fire. The combined fire is being battled on all fronts, but it is out of control." They showed a map, and the wildfire was headed right in our direction. "Be calm Joyce. Prepare," I told myself. I called Ed at work to tell him what was happening. My mouth turned to cotton as I asked him if there was anything in the house that he wanted me to take.

First I got Mary, Jolie and Doug into the back seat of the car. I turned the car to face the street for a quick getaway. Then I asked Charlie to get the garden hose and carefully get on the roof of the barn and start hosing it down. Back in the house, I worked quickly. I took the silver chest and threw it into the swimming pool, took down the portrait of Dad's grandfather and put it in the trunk of the car. I grabbed Jolie's new school clothes, threw them on top of the painting (don't ask; I knew that Carol Ann had just purchased them and I didn't want them to burn).

In the distance, coming up the canyon behind our house, I could see red flames. I panicked and called to Charlie, "Get off the roof now! Run to the car!"

Our two standard poodles and five puppies were barking in their pen. I wrapped the puppies in a blanket and led the dogs to the car, where the four children sat wide-eyed. Lucky it was a station wagon! How would I get the donkey out of the corral and hitched to the back of the car? I took a carrot out of the refrigerator and ran to the corral, tied a rope around the donkey's neck, showed him the carrot and pulled on the robe to get him to come out of the corral. He wouldn't budge. I keep pulling frantically. Charlie ran from the car to help.

"Go get back in the car, honey!"

"But I want to help."

"Now! In the car!"

The flames were getting closer and I was terrified. I pulled on the donkey and looked at the sky. The sun was covered with black smoke and the sky was an angry shade of red and orange. I felt like Scarlet O'Hara in "Gone with the Wind." If I didn't get out of there immediately, we would all perish! I dropped the rope and ran as fast as I could to the car. I hoped the donkey would run toward the road for safety. But now I had to get the children out of harm's way. As I neared the car, the children were yelling, "Hurry up! Hurry up!!"

I pulled out of the driveway onto the street. As we passed a neighbor's house, a frantic woman holding a fur coat in one hand and a chicken in the other waved the chicken in the air for us to stop. I slammed on the brakes. She dropped her fur coat and jumped into the crowded back seat with the chicken. We were off!

I was OK until Charlie asked, "Mommy, will my Halloween costume burn?" Suddenly the reality hit me. We took our neighbor with her chicken to her relative's home, then drove to a friend's house and waited for Ed to meet us there. The children were all being very brave. I wondered what the future would bring. Ed met us at our friend's house, where we sat huddled in front of the TV, watching the news. A few hours after dark, the news reporter gave an update on the fire. "Several homes have burned, including the home of actors Edward Mallory and Joyce Bulifant in Granada Hills."

What a sinking feeling that was. I said, "At least we're all safe." An hour later, after trying to comfort each other, Ed and I drove back to look at the damage.

In school I had been taught that if you are ever in a burning building, you should close the doors to the rooms and leave the lights on so that firemen can see if anyone needs to be rescued. The lesson stuck in my mind, and I had done that before we left our house. Hearts sinking and preparing for the worst, we rounded the corner to our street. In the dark we could smell the stench of smoldering ashes and were able to make out clouds of smoke rising from the burned fields. It seemed as if we were driving through the set of a horror movie. We drove a little further down our street and in the distance saw the lights on in our home. The reporter was wrong. It was still standing, shining through the darkness.

The house was saved, but what about our smoldering marriage? Ed wasn't interested in me sexually and I began to feel I wasn't attractive or desirable. When I tried to talk to him about it, he responded angrily, "The theatre is my temple! That's the most important thing to me."

I did just what you shouldn't do when a marriage is in trouble; I asked Ed if he would like to have a baby. He wanted to have a son. On one of the very few occasions that we made love, I became pregnant.

Since we weren't usually intimate, he wasn't aware of my monthly cycle. This meant I could surprise him with the happy news that we were going to have a baby. On our second anniversary as he sat at the breakfast table I gave him a present, a pair of baby booties with a note, "Your real gift will be here in 7 months!"

He looked at me in confusion. "I don't understand."

"We're going to have a baby!" I said with a big grin on my face, as I wrapped my arms around him.

"It better be a boy." He shrugged me off and picked up his cup of coffee.

I was able to work all through my pregnancy. On the first "Bill Cosby Show," Bill played a high school basketball coach and I played the school guidance counselor, a recurring role. One day on the set towards the end of my pregnancy, I was standing off-camera, ready to enter. The cameraman said, "Joyce, I can see you, stand back a little more." I thought I was standing back far enough, but I looked down and saw it was my growing belly that was sticking out. It looked as if I had gained a lot of weight.

"Please," I begged the writers, "please write in the script that Mrs. Patterson is pregnant." They kept forgetting. It was time to put my foot down. "Okay, now you have to say I'm pregnant. My belly is making an entrance before I am!"

Since Roger and I shared so many of the same friends, there were times we would be invited to the same parties. One of those occasions was our friend Norman's wedding. Roger and I managed to spend a little time talking to each other, sharing polite greetings. I managed to keep a cool heart, because I was married and Roger was living with JoAnne.

The time for my baby's delivery drew near. Dolores, Norman's wife, and some other friends, gave me a baby shower. Roger's girlfriend, JoAnne Worley, was also invited. I was delighted that JoAnne came to the shower. It gave me a chance to get to know her better. In the past we had only exchanged friendly chit-chat. She seemed to be a nice, fun person. She gave me a beautiful quilt for the baby's crib. I was glad that everyone could be friendly.

At the time of my pregnancy, not only was I doing the Cosby show, but I was also a recurring character, Marie, on "The Mary Tyler Moore Show." I played the wife of the very kind and sweet actor, Gavin McLeod, who played Murray. They wrote in my pregnancy. As a matter of fact, I had a call while I was in labor asking if I would come in for a table reading because I was in the following week's show.

With Gavin MacLeod and Mary Tyler Moore

"Not right now," I groaned from the labor room.

I had gone into labor at 4 am. We lived quite a distance from St. John's hospital, where Mary had been born. I thought we shouldn't dilly-dally getting there, since this was my third child and they seemed to come more quickly each time. We drove through the dark to the hospital. Of course the minute we got there and I was in the labor room, the contractions stopped.

Carol Ann arrived about breakfast time, and I visited with Ed and Carol Ann in the waiting room. Carol Ann said to Ed, "Now, you stop this nonsense about wanting a boy." She patted his knee. "You know you just want a healthy baby."

"No, I want a boy!" He went off to smoke a cigarette.

I was back in the labor room and Carol Ann and Ed had gone down to have lunch. The doctor sat in the corner of my room reading the newspaper. He folded the paper, stood up, looked at me and said impatiently, "You sure are taking your time. I'm going down for lunch."

The minute everyone left, the strongest labor pain hit and I felt I was ready to push.

"Nurse," I said politely. "Oh, Nurse."

"Nurse!" I screamed from my room to the hallway. She came running. I said, "I'm ready to push, the baby is coming!"

She said, officiously, "Oh no, I just checked you. You aren't dilated enough."

Measuring each word, I said, "I-have-had-two other-babies-and-this-one-is-coming ... NOW!"

The next thing I knew, I was rushed to the delivery room and then I blacked out. I had wanted to be awake for my baby's delivery. They must have panicked because the doctor wasn't there, so they gave me a shot to put me out. Shortly, after I came to, a little bundle with a blue cap was put gently in my arms. A son!

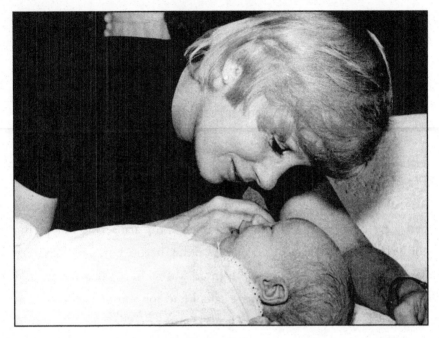

A new love

We named our son Edward John Mallory. Edward, after his father, John after St. John. Ed was Catholic, and Catholics are supposed to have a saint's name as part of their name. We would call him John.

Sonnet Hill Farm was adding a nursery that wasn't completed in time for John's arrival. Mary's room was part of the remodel, so she was sleeping on the sofa in the den. John's bassinet was near my side of the bed in our bedroom.

On February 9, 1971, just before the sun was about to slip through the curtains of our bedroom, a huge rattling sound and a loud explosion, like a bomb, shook the house so hard that it threw Ed out of bed and me on top of him.

I thought we were being bombed! Or was it the end of the world? Trying to get to my feet, I fell off balance. Blue lights like streaks of lighting were flashing outside the windows. Ed, on his feet, reached for John in his bassinet. "It's an earthquake."

He had John safe in his arms, and now I needed to get to Charlie and Mary. Feeling my way in the dark toward the bedroom door, I tripped on something blocking the door. It was a large mirror that had been thrown across the door. I grabbed it and shoved it out of the way. Charlie was calling from his room by the kitchen. "Mommy, Mommy?"

"Charlie, honey." I tried to sound as calm as I could. "Don't walk on the floor! Step on the chairs to get to us. There's broken glass all over." I reached Charlie and took his hand to help him off the chair and we headed to the den to check on Mary, who was sitting up in the sofa bed. I sat down next to her and held her in my arms. She was crying softly, brave little girl, only five years old. Charlie, now ten, was very good at covering his fears. All I wanted was to have my arms around my children and know they were safe. I had John in one arm, an arm around Mary, with Charlie sitting as close as possible.

We did everything you shouldn't. We were sitting on the sofa bed where Mary had been sleeping, but we were under a glass window. Ed lit candles, a real hazard. In the next shake, they could fall over and start a fire. We knew nothing about turning off the gas. Another big shake came. We held tighter to each other. Ed took over in a commanding voice, "We should go in the field behind the house."

In a nice, calming motherly voice, I shouted, "NO! The earth will open up and swallow us!" Fear had found its way into my very being.

Ed turned on the TV in the den. A newscaster was sitting on a stool in the parking lot of NBC with just one light on him. He announced that a 7.1 Earthquake had struck in Sylmar. We were very near the epicenter. Afterquakes kept coming. The news announcer said the blue flashes came from telephone wires that had snapped, scattered small fires had started because of gas lines breaking, several freeways had collapsed, and many buildings had slid off their foundation. There was going to be an evacuation because there was fear of a dam breaking.

Dear Gavin MacLeod, who played my husband on "The Mary Tyler Moore Show," was worried about us and appeared at our door with hot dogs from Nathan's. Such a sweet friend!

I asked Ed if we could take the children and stay in a hotel closer to L.A., where there wasn't so much shaking. I couldn't even think about going to bed in our own home that night. We packed and spent a few nights in a hotel. After the shaking settled down a bit, we went back home.

The ground may have stopped shaking, but our marriage was still on shaky ground. It seemed as if our marriage had become a soap opera: fire, earthquake, and Ed's yelling until all hours. But the children and work kept me busy and a wonderful baby boy helped me try to focus on my blessings.

Ed continued to drink and swear. He often shouted, "God Damn It!" and was always irritated with one thing or another. When Christmas came, he calmed down a bit. As a surprise I had an office built for him in the barn. They worked on it while he was at the studio, and I found an old roll-top desk for him. Christmas morning I covered his eyes and led him to the barn. When he saw his surprise, he hugged me and cried. He could be so endearing at times.

Mother was visiting us. We had large family dinners, and the house was happy. When Mother left a few days after Christmas, we rented a house with Carol Ann and her family in Big Bear for New Year's. Our friends from Theatre East rented a home nearby. I didn't want to join them because I had the children to look after. Besides, I didn't want to spend New Year's Eve watching Ed get drunk or see Roger with JoAnne.

On New Year's Day, Charlie, Doug, Jolie and Mary wanted to toboggan. Lee and Carol Ann took them to a toboggan hill. Before they left I gathered them in the kitchen and while tying a scarf around

Mary's neck, I gave them the toboggan rules. I looked at their expectant faces.

"Never, NEVER stick your foot out to stop. Just roll over to the side in the snow. You'll break your leg if you stick it out. Promise me."

"We promise."

"OK, off you go." I waved goodbye and started clearing the lunch dishes. Then I put John, now almost one, down for his nap.

A few hours later I decided to go to the hill so I could watch the children. They were having a great time. "Come on Mommy, take a ride with us!" I sat on the toboggan with Mary between my legs and Charlie behind me. We started down the hill, going faster and faster. I saw the road looming in front of us and panicked. Out came my leg to stop us.

Snap crackle and pop!—I heard my leg break in several places. The toboggan had turned over, and the children and I had fallen out. Charlie tried to get out from under me. "Hey, Mom, you're on top of me."

"I'm sorry," I said, and passed out in the snow.

When I came to in the mountain's First Aid cabin, I heard a man's voice. "You'll have to take her down to San Bernardino hospital to get that leg set. I'll give her a shot of Demerol to help the pain while you drive her down." I was in a fog; in my haze, I thought I saw Roger standing by the bed. (For years I thought I had been dreaming. I found out much later that he had heard about the accident and had rushed to see if I was all right. It wasn't a dream!)

My cast finally came off. Life went on. It was almost Christmas again, followed by John's second birthday. Ed continued to drink. One day I took John clothes shopping with me. He was a cute little fellow, fair, blue-eyed, with a mop of blonde curls. While I was going through a rack of dresses, a lady came up to John in his stroller and leaned down to say, "What a beautiful little boy you are."

"Shut up, God damn it!" came out of that little rosebud of a mouth. I fell into the dress rack, afraid to come out. He had certainly heard his father say that often enough. I think that may have been his first sentence.

At home things were becoming more difficult. I was afraid that Ed's scenes were upsetting the children. Sometimes Ed would say he was going to kill himself. He seemed to have such demons. Was I one of them? I didn't know if he was angry and disappointed with himself or me. I started marking the level of vodka in the bottles with a pencil. Maybe I would be able to tell, when he was on one of his dark tirades, if the alcohol was causing the problem.

Because of Ed's threats to kill himself, whenever I came home from the market and the children were with me, I asked them to wait in the car a minute, until I went in and checked. One Saturday when Ed was home alone and I returned from the store, I walked by the kitchen window and was shocked to see Ed drinking straight out of a vodka bottle. Another time, when I walked into our bedroom, I saw him on his knees in front of his cabinet hiding a bottle. I pretended that I didn't see. I didn't want to embarrass him.

I was always very concerned about the children. Could they hear Ed yelling at night? I would plead with him to be quiet, but still he would carry on. Adding to that concern were the children's weekends with Jimmy. Was he getting drunk as well? He promised me there would always be someone to look after the children when they were with him. But what kinds of people were hanging around?

One night after tucking Charlie into bed, I sat beside him. He had seemed a bit withdrawn and sad. "Everything okay?"

"I feel like a puzzle with a piece missing."

"Why do you think that is?" I took his hand.

"I don't know, I just do."

I kissed him good-night. "If you ever need to talk, I'm right here to listen. I love you so much. Good night, honey."

He rolled over in bed and with a heavy heart, I turned out the light. I never said anything bad about their father to Charlie and Mary because I remembered how awful I had felt when my mother said bad things about my father, and how I disliked her for it. I wanted them to feel close to their father and make their own judgments later, as adults.

One day, when I was discussing the children with Jimmy on the phone, I asked him if he might help pay for ballet lessons for Mary. There was very little money from him for their support and I hoped he might help a little more.

"Let them eat alfalfa."

I never asked him again.

Jimmy got a series that was going to shoot in Hawaii, "Hawaii Five-0." He would play the role of detective Danny "Danno" Williams. Jim wanted the children to visit him in the summer for a month, much longer than I wanted. He said he would have a responsible person look after them. After the sad memory of not being able to see my own father very often while I was growing up, I felt it was important for the children to see their father. As long as they had someone to look after them, I tried to convince myself it would be all right. But it was painful to think of Charlie and Mary being away for such a long time. Putting those two little ones on the plane to fly alone across the Pacific Ocean, stay with Jimmy and be taken care of by someone I didn't know scared me to death. I was able to go on the plane with them to hug and kiss them goodbye. Putting on a brave face and a big smile, I told them what a great time they would have. But when I turned to leave I couldn't hold back the tears. I walked away and couldn't look back.

I had to trust Jimmy's judgment. My mother however, had a different view—she suddenly decided to move to Hawaii. She would be there to keep an eye on the children when they were with Jimmy. God bless her! She bought an apartment right across the street from Jimmy's. One morning Jimmy went out to stretch on his veranda, and Mother waved at him from her apartment. The next day when she went out to give Jim a morning wave, she noticed a long bamboo shade that blocked her view.

With the children gone and just Ed, John and me at home, I thought things might get better. There was less going on and I could give my complete attention to Ed and John. Things got worse. Ed's ranting and raving, drinking and yelling put me on edge. I hoped John in his nursery couldn't hear his father's shouts that lasted late into the night. His anger wasn't aimed at me—it was his work, friends, family, the whole world.

One night when Ed was carrying on in the bedroom, shouting about one thing and another, I tried to calm him down by saying the world wasn't as bad as he thought. Although the subject was very difficult for me to bring up, I mentioned our lack of sex. I was afraid he would just become more upset at the mention of sex, but I felt unattractive, and I felt we needed help.

"Ed, I feel so sad that we don't make love. What's wrong? Can we talk about it?" The words stuck in my throat but I forced them out. I was sitting up in bed with my arms around my knees. Ed was pacing up and down like an actor taking center stage. He stopped pacing and turned towards me with a quizzical look.

"When I was in college my roommate made an altar with my picture on it, an altar to me. Strange huh? I don't know… maybe I'm gay. Do you think I'm gay?"

I thought carefully before I spoke. "Ed, only you would know that. If you are, it's all right. It's important that you are true to yourself. I just want you to be happy."

I wondered: maybe I was a desirable woman, but Ed just wasn't attracted to me?

A few days later, Marietta Hartley gave me a book that changed my life. I do believe in angels; they come to us in all different ways. This time it was Marietta. The book was *The Co-Alcoholic*.

I sat on my bed reading. When I finished the last page, I closed the book and sat deep in thought. "It's a book about me." I said it out loud. Stunned, I realized I was a big part of Ed's problem and probably Jimmy's too. Certainly my own.

What should I do? I must tell Ed our problems weren't entirely his fault. I had allowed his drinking and bad behavior. I had allowed my children to live in a home with constant tension and I had lived without marital love. It's my fault, I kept saying to myself. Now I have to fix myself and help my children. I didn't want to get a divorce. Two divorces! Two mistakes, partly mine. I kept thinking, what do I do? What do I do?

The book gave some suggestions. Maybe things would work out, if I just explained everything to Ed. If I asked him to get help and he did, we could possibly be together again as a family. But he didn't want to get help. The drinking continued. One night I told Ed I wasn't helping him by staying married. I was concerned for the children and for myself. I wanted a divorce.

The next day I dragged sadness and worry with me to work. I tried to smile when I reached the studio where I was working on the series, "Love thy Neighbor" with Ron Masak. I had confided in him about what was going on.

**With Ron Masak, Janet MacLachlan,
Harrison Page in "Love thy Neighbor"**

Later in the day, Ed called. "Hello, Joyce. I want you to know this is J Day."

"What? Ed, I don't understand."

"You'll see. Just remember it's J day."

He sounded very strange and I was worried. The rest of the day was difficult to get through. I wanted work to be over so I could get home to the children. When I walked into the house and started toward our bedroom, I saw a large note taped to the door, "J Day," and beneath that, "Knock on the door-put the children in their rooms-knock on the door again-count to 50-slowly open the door."

What in the world was going on? I walked through the living room to make sure the children were in their rooms and noticed all the plants, flowers and candles from the mantle and the dining room table were missing. Oh, no, he wants to have a romantic dinner in the bedroom. I was tired and I didn't want to be lured back into a very bad situation.

I knocked on the door, counted to 50 and opened the bedroom door. The room was filled with flowers and plants. Every candle in the house was burning. Ed was laid out like a corpse on the bed wearing the suit he was married in, with dead flowers stuck in the lapel. His face was painted white and his hands were folded across his chest. Above his head was a huge painted sign "IF YOU LEAVE ME I WILL DIE." A bottle of champagne and two champagne flutes were on the night-stand. On the record player, Patti Page sang, "Is that all there is?"

After his many threats of suicide, my reaction to this scene was horror! I was furious and terribly upset. I tried to lift the needle off the record, but it skidded across, making a terrible screeching sound. I yelled and cried at the same time, "This isn't funny! It isn't nice! Get up! Get up!" I kept yelling and sobbing at the same time.

I filed for divorce.

One of the most difficult things was to tell my dear friend, Lillian Gish, whom I considered my "Fairy Godmother," that I was getting divorced. She and I had become very close. To me, she was an angel on earth who could do no wrong. I didn't want to be seen as a failure again in Helen's eyes, or my mother's eyes, or the eyes of all my friends.

When I visited Lillian in New York, we often sat together in her apartment and talked about spiritual matters over the champagne and Godiva chocolates she always served. These were very special times with her that I cherished. When Helen, her best friend, was upset with me and not very kind, Lillian would say, "It's just the Irish in her, dear. Pay no mind." Lillian, through everything, was always kind and loving to me, as was her good friend, Jim Frasier. I hated to call and tell her I was getting divorced... again! Sitting by the bed, I held the phone, trying to summon my courage. When I got the nerve, I quickly dialed her number and waited. When she answered, I spilled the news out, like a gambler at a crap table, as quickly as possible.

There was a long pause and then her sweet and loving voice answered, "Darling, maybe you're like me. Maybe you're not meant to be married. Just do as I do. Love them and leave them."

*

I sold our home and helped Ed find a rented house in the Hollywood Hills. Together we furnished his new place. I had enough money left, after giving Ed half the profit from the sale of our house (even thought he had no investment in it), to buy a modest house in a nice family neighborhood in North Hollywood, close to the studios. That was important because I needed to work. There was no alimony from Ed and very little support for Charlie and Mary from Jim, except for medical and school expenses.

I was busy the next six months fixing up our home and working (thank heaven). Ed would come by occasionally to see John. He was always nice and I never saw him drunk during that time. Ed told me he had stopped drinking. I was happy for him; he looked better and he didn't seem as anxious and stressed.

One evening, after eating dinner with us, he gave me a gift and told me not to open it until Christmas, which was just around the corner. This was a Christmas I wasn't looking forward to because the children were scheduled to go on a trip with Jimmy right after we opened our gifts on Christmas morning.

After opening our gifts, I looked around the living room—Santa's workshop gone amok, stockings opened, candy canes spilled on the floor, wrapping paper and ribbons strewn around the room. The children were happily playing with their gifts. John, three years old, really enjoyed Christmas and was exhausted from the excitement. When it was his naptime, I settled him in bed and heard the doorbell ring. It was Jimmy to pick up Charlie and Mary, who were excited to see him. Their bags were packed and ready by the front door. Jimmy and I exchanged a hug and I handed off my precious little ones to him with a big pretend smile on my face.

"Have a wonderful time, I'll miss you. I love you."

Little Mary, now almost eight, looked just as cute as could be, her blonde pigtails tied with bows. She reached up on her tiptoes to give me a hug, "Love you, Mommy." I bent down to hug and kiss her. Oh, how I hated to let her go!

Charlie, now in his first teen year, picked up his suitcase, "Love ya, Mom."

Hugging him and brushing back his hair, I said, "I love you, honey." I watched them walk to the waiting car, waved goodbye, and closed the door. After cleaning up the debris, I went to the kitchen to make a cup of tea. A nice hot cup tea and a warm bath always seemed to help during lonely, sad times, and this was one of them.

I sat in my grandmother's chair by the fire sipping my tea. I opened Ed's gift. What a surprise! It was a record with a special cover, "Butterflies and Summer Nights" by Edward Mallory, sung by Bill Hayes. It was a fully orchestrated song written for me, along with a note that said, "Let's try again." Two tickets for a cruise to Mexico were pasted to the note. The divorce wouldn't be final for another six months, and Ed hadn't had a drink for five months. Well, why not? Carol Ann said she would look after John. It seemed like perfect timing, and maybe we could put the pieces back together again.

The trip was wonderful! Ed didn't drink at all and there was a night or two of making love. We decided we could make this work again. Having had some counseling in the last six months, I set boundaries: no drinking and no yelling. Ed agreed and we renewed our vows to each other in the back of a taxicab in Mexico.

We bought a house, a beautiful place that actor Walter Brennan had owned. It had a brick courtyard and pool, a step-down living room with rafters and a big fireplace. Summer arrived and everyone was happy; all was going well. John was with us and Charlie and Mary were in Hawaii with Jimmy for a month.

One especially warm night, the phone rang.

Jimmy's frantic voice, "Joyce, have you heard from Charlie?"

"What, no. What's wrong?"

"He's run away."

"I don't understand. Why? What happened?"

"He got in a fight with my wife." (Jimmy had remarried.)

"What do you mean, a fight?" I was beside myself with worry. What in the world was going on and where was Charlie?

"He pushed her and he's run away. Can you call your mother to see if she knows where he is?"

"I'll call her right away. That just doesn't sound like Charlie at all. I'll call Mother right away, and call you back." I hung up in a panic. My son was missing and I was an ocean away, not able to look for him or help him. Ed came running in. "What's wrong?"

I told him Charlie had run away.

I called Mother. "Mother, do you know where Charlie is?"

"What? What do you mean? Doesn't Jimmy know where he is?"

"No, something happened and he's run away. If you hear from him, no matter what time, please call me. I'm so frightened."

"What happened?"

"Jimmy said Charlie hit or pushed his wife. I don't know. I'm just so afraid."

"Try not to worry, honey, I'll call you or you call me, no matter what time. OK?"

I turned to Ed and the tears came. "I have to call Jim."

I asked if Jimmy had heard from Charlie. He said he hadn't. I asked him to call the police. Jimmy said he wanted to wait a while in the hopes Charlie would show up.

"Please call me right away when you know something. I just don't understand what happened."

"Yeah." He hung up.

I couldn't go to bed. I sat in the den staring at the phone and willing it to ring. Several hours went by. The sound of the phone startled me. It was Jimmy; Charlie had climbed in the back of Jim's car and fallen asleep. I would learn the true story from Charlie later, when he came home.

Thank heavens, the children finally came home from Hawaii. I never felt entirely comfortable while they were with Jimmy, but it helped to know that Mother was nearby. Once at home, Charlie explained what the altercation had been with Jim's wife. Charlie said he pushed her away because she was smashing his head into a wall. He said he never tried to hit her. He had run away and hid in his father's car to stop from getting hurt. Many years later, I learned that drugs had been involved, and not on Charlie's part. A few weeks later, Charlie showed Ed and me a picture of a naked woman in a magazine. He said his dad had shown him the picture and had said something very crude. His head bent, Charlie closed the magazine. He looked up and said, "I never want to treat women the way my dad does." Charlie was learning about his father. He was growing up and it was sad that he had to learn the very dark side.

A "Mother and Son" trip was in order. It was important, I thought, to spend individual time alone with each child. It was always a treat for me, and I hoped it made them feel special. Charlie and I headed for a cabin in Yosemite. What a peaceful place, just what we needed. I needed a break from Ed, who had started to drink again. He had terrible back spasms, for which he took muscle relaxants. The combination of pills and alcohol caused his old behavior to return. It was best to keep on the divorce track. I realized I couldn't hold the family together.

Ed moved out and I put the house on the market. This time I had put the house in my name alone. He was drinking and smoking away most of his money from "Days of Our Lives," and rumor had it he was becoming difficult on the set. Poor Ed, I did love him and I felt so sorry for his misery.

Back into much-needed counseling for me. I read lots of self-help books and tried to make life as stress-free as possible for me and the children.

*

I had been doing a lot of game shows, including "Password." Being dyslexic, I was pretty good at "Password" because I always had to think of one word to get to another. It was the perfect game show for me. When they produced "Celebrity Password," I won! We were playing for our favorite charities; mine was a center for abused children. I also appeared on the "$25,000 Pyramid."

The show I did most often was "Match Game," known for its risqué banter. I was teased a lot on that show because I gave such silly

With Susan, Daddy, Jeannie, Linda and Jackie

answers, often because I couldn't spell the correct word and was too embarrassed to give it a try. Oh dear, I did seem to get in a lot of trouble on "Match Game!"

One time, the question was about a dentist. When it was my turn, I asked the producer, who was standing behind the camera, if it was all right to tell a true story that had run in the Chicago newspaper. He nodded, yes. So off I went. "Well, a dentist raped a girl and the headline said 'Dentist Fills Wrong Cavity.'" The audience went wild with laughter.

Another sentence we had to complete: the head undertaker was upset with his assistant because when he buried Mr. Smith, his _____ was hanging out of the coffin. I called Gene over to me and asked, "How stiff was he?"

I was a bit embarrassed by my outbursts, but the audience seemed to love it and the producers kept asking me back.

It was always a chore to try to get up the stairs to my dressing room without running into Gene Rayburn, the host of the show. The stairway was narrow, and Gene would try to plant a big wet kiss on me as I passed by. I sure didn't like it but tried not to offend him, so I waited until I got to my dressing room before saying "Ugh!" and wiping it away.

The three seats on the top row of the celebrity panel consisted of a guest star in the first seat; Brett Somers, dry, caustic and very funny, in the middle seat; and Charles Nelson Reilly, next to Brett, added his gay, flamboyant, sophisticated humor. The bottom seats were reserved for a guest, usually a lovely young actress; Richard Dawson, British and also the host of "Family Feud," claimed to know everything and thought he was God's gift to women; and the sixth seat in the lower level was where I sat, in the place sometimes occupied by Betty White, Patti Deutsch, and Fannie Flagg.

Charles Nelson Reilly was hilarious and also fun during our dinner breaks. Brett Sommers became a good friend but hated to visit me in the "dreaded valley," as she called it. Richard Dawson was a different story. Oh my, he kept asking me to go out with him. I really didn't want to, but since I sat next to him on the show, I thought it would be polite to go for dinner one night. The afternoon of our dinner date, he called to say he had let his staff go for the evening. He would pick me up in the valley and drive me to his house in Bel Air, where he would prepare dinner. Oh NO!!! I didn't know what to say. His plan spelled trouble. I hung up and immediately called my friend Peggy. She made a super suggestion, to tell him that Mary wasn't feeling well and I needed to stay in the neighborhood. When I telephoned and told him, he hung up on me, and that was the end of that date. The next time I was on "Match Game," he pushed me as we entered the stage and my head banged into the heavy "Match Game" sign hanging from the ceiling. Not my favorite fella!

＊

My friend Eileen and I went searching for my next home. We came upon an open house, an English Tudor. As we walked through the house, I pointed out to Eileen what could be done to make it more charming. "See how much better it would look to take this wall out and make one large room. Oh, now this bedroom would be great if you put in French doors leading to the garden. Don't you think? And if you replaced this ugly carpet with used brick, don't you think it would look much better?"

Someone behind me asked, "Are you an interior designer? Your ideas for this house are really good. I've had several designers come by to give me ideas, but I really like yours. You've come up with things no one else has."

I turned around. "Pardon?"

"I'm looking for a designer for several homes I'm building. Are you a designer? Would you be interested?"

I was startled. "Oh well, I'm not…" Before I could finish, my friend Eileen piped up, "Yes, she does great work. You should see the home she lives in now!"

I gave Eileen a shocked look.

The man said, "Let me give you my card."

Eileen grabbed it from his hand. "Thank you. We'll call you." I was still standing with my mouth open. She hushed me and pulled me out of the house.

"Eileen, what in the world!"

"Don't you need extra money? Do you have a job right now?"

"No, but...."

"Well, you're going to have one now! You're really great at decorating houses. So this is what we're going to do. We'll call him and invite him to your house so he can see what you can do."

That very evening, the gentleman came to the house and made a deal with me to do the interior design for a new house he was building and to work on several remodels of spec homes. What a friend Eileen was! So between acting jobs, I had a way to keep making money. I really enjoyed the homes he gave me to remodel. Working with the architects was so creative. There was never any need to say I had no credentials—they never asked. What I did have was a lot of nerve! I changed an inexpensive Spanish home with gold specks in the stucco to an English-style country home. The builder ended up making more profit than he expected. With my help, the English country style became his trademark. He did very well and I felt very proud.

I found a house in Sherman Oaks, a charming tree-lined neighborhood, with a school a few blocks away for Mary and a nursery school for John. Charlie was attending nearby Harvard School for Boys. The house, a cottage really, had a picket fence covered with roses and a swing hanging from a tree in the front yard. French doors in the living room looked out onto a lovely pool. The children would have their own rooms, with trees outside their windows.

A rock group, Deep Purple, owned the house. The realtor said I could go by the house before they moved out to see if I might like to buy some of their furniture. On Sunday I walked over wet grass to reach the front door. I rang the doorbell and waited. A man with flowing black hair and a long purple robe opened the door.

"Got any grass on you?"

I inspected the sole of my shoe to wipe off any grass. My foot was halfway up when it dawned on me he meant a different kind of grass.

"No, so sorry."

He showed me into the house. I purchased a sofa that would look elegant with my English hutch.

After we moved in, I had John's room wallpapered with pictures of trains. Mary's wallpaper had rosebuds, and Charlie, who was about to be a sophomore in high school, had his walls painted his favorite color blue.

It seemed as if my life ricocheted from big house to little house, little house to big house. Funny, it was the cozy little houses that seemed just right. I traded in my station wagon for a used Mercedes and felt quite the successful actress, but I wasn't feeling like a successful mother. I didn't want my children to experience the pain I had felt as a child, separated from my father.

Ed knew how important I thought it was for children of divorced parents to have as much time as possible with each parent. John, just three years old, was sad because Ed wasn't spending very much time with him.

One night while John was eating his dinner, he took a spoonful of food, and lifted it to the empty chair next to him. Puzzled, I said, "John, Honey, what are you doing?"

His little sad face looked up at me. "I'm feeding my Daddy."

I wrote a song for John called "Why's My Daddy Gone?" I wanted John to understand that his father had not left him, but I had asked him to leave. I didn't want John to feel abandoned by his father, as I had felt as a child. The lyrics were:

"Why's my Daddy gone, my little fellow said today.
He doesn't love me, that's why he went away.

Oh, no, little fellow, your Daddy loves you so.

He went away 'cause your Mama asked him to go.

Oh, my little fellow, please try to understand.

Come close to your Mama, let me hold your hand.

I love you, little fellow, with your eyes so soft and blue.

You look like your Daddy, and I guess I love him too.

Oh, my little fellow, someday when you're all grown,

you'll have a love to call your very own.

And dear little fellow, please be good and true.

Don't hurt your little fellow like your Mama hurt you."

The Thanksgiving after Ed and I were divorced, Laura Mako, Helen's good friend, invited Charlie, Mary and me for Thanksgiving at her home. What a kind gesture. We arrived among many guests. Laura, an interior designer, is the consummate hostess, and her lovely home is welcoming. It was a rainy day and the children and I arrived all bundled up and wet. Helen greeted the children with warm affection, while I was given barely a polite nod. When we went in to dinner, there were many round tables. Charlie was holding my hand and Mary the other. Helen said, "Joyce, the children are sitting beside me. Your table is over there." I let go of their hands and went to a table on the other side of the room, as if I had been banished to Siberia. The cold shoulder Helen had given me made me feel wretched.

There were several times that followed when Helen asked me to bring the children. Off she would go with them, leaving me in the background. It was hurtful, but I wanted the children to be able to share time with their Grammy. I always held out hope that she would love me again one day.

*

I was not the least bit interested in dating. Happily, I sequestered myself in the evenings at home with my children. On the few occasions when I went out in the evening, I told Rose, our housekeeper, to make sure lights were out early for John and Mary, but Charlie could study as long as he needed. Charlie had become a good student and a terrific young man. He drove classmates to school to earn money for gas and dates. I was so proud of him.

During this period I was seeing a therapist, still trying to put together pieces of my life. I wanted to make certain I wouldn't marry again without first understanding why I had chosen the men I had married. It was time to fix me. And boy, did I need fixing! The therapist suggested I learn more about my father and his marriage to my mother.

I decided to go to Florida and visit my father, whom I hadn't seen for almost seventeen years. Charlie was in school, and John was too young for the trip, but little Mary, age eight, would go with me. Mother said she would come and help Rose, our housekeeper, look after the boys for two weeks.

On the way we visited my Aunt Billie in Baltimore. I was happy to see her again, after all the wonderful times we had together when I was a young girl. She and my grandmother had felt my mother was too strict with me, so naturally I loved her. Aunt Billie and my mother didn't get along at all; Mother was a bit pretentious, while Aunt Billie was more down-to-earth.

As we landed in Florida, all the memories of my father, my Prince Charming, came flooding back to me. In just a few hours I would see him. Swinging onto a narrow road, I saw a tin mailbox with

BULIFANT neatly printed on it. My excitement mounted! Mary and I got of our rented car and walked toward the house hand in hand, gravel crunching under our feet.

Daddy opened the screen door and his big arms enveloped me. Jackie, his wife, hugged Mary. "Well, well, well, I'll be a humdinger," Daddy said, "You're a sight for sore eyes." Daddy reached down to hug Mary and then held her at arms' length. "You look just like your Mommy did when she was a little girl. Y'all come on in, now. What can I get you?"

Mary and I, both in a daze, walked into their neat, cheery home.

"Jackie and the girls have made up a good supper for us, but first, will you do me a favor before we wash up? I want to give thanks to the Lord."

The seven of us held hands in a circle—Daddy, Jackie, Linda and Susan (my twin sisters) and Jeannie (my youngest sister), Mary and I. Mary's little hand was in mine, and Daddy's big hand held my other hand tightly. Daddy said, "Let's bow our heads a minute. Dear Lord, thank you for bringing Joyce and Mary to us safely. We're so happy they're here."

Daddy lifted his head and looked at me through misty eyes. I gave him a hug and felt at home. On the last night of our visit, after supper, Daddy was washing dishes and I was drying. I managed to tell him something about my failed marriages. Then I hesitantly asked, "Why did you and mother get divorced?"

Daddy dried his hands on the dishtowel. He looked at me. I stopped drying. I could tell it wasn't easy for him to answer.

"Honey, I had a hard time at work. I couldn't write out reports. You see, I couldn't spell. I was in charge of a thousand men and at the end of each day, I was supposed to write out a report. I tried doing a little song and dance around the issue, said it'd be easier and faster if I just told my boss what happened instead of writing it down. He wouldn't accept that. I got real frustrated and I started drinking. And I guess maybe I wasn't so nice to your mother. I take most of the blame for the breakup. Your mother was a nice lady."

Was that why I chose men who drank? I never saw my Daddy drunk, at least I had no such memory. What I did learn was that my Daddy was dyslexic, just like me and John.

*

At home after the trip, the children and I got busy decorating the house for Christmas. John, now five, was given the task of putting up the manger scene. He carefully unwrapped the manger and then unrolled the figurines of Mary and Joseph from tissue paper in our Christmas box. Then he found the angel, the three wise men, the shepherds and all the animals.

I went into my bedroom and suddenly heard him cry, "Mommy, Mommy, I can't find the baby Jesus!"

Rushing back to the living room, I took each piece of tissue paper and searched through the box, but the baby Jesus was nowhere to be found. John started crying. Suddenly my motherly brain kicked in. I kneeled down and wiped away his tears.

"Of course the baby Jesus isn't here. He wasn't born until Christmas." His little face broke into a smile. "Oh, that's right, Mommy."

We set up the manger with all the figurines except the baby Jesus. I made a mental note to be sure to buy a baby Jesus to place in the manger on Christmas Eve. But with my work schedule plus Christmas on my mind, I forgot.

On Christmas Eve, Charlie, Mary, John and I kneeled in prayer at All Saint's Church for the special children's service. The minister was telling the story of the birth of Jesus.

"Jesus!" I suddenly remembered the baby Jesus figure for our manger. I started to panic; there would be no place late on Christmas Eve to buy a baby Jesus. I looked at John's little hands folded in prayer and knew how upset he would be. I felt so awful, I didn't hear a word of the rest of the service.

When we left the church, the minister reached in his pocket and gave each child a gift. I saw that one child got a donkey, another a camel. Next came a shepherd, and as John reached out for his gift, the minister handed him the baby Jesus.

John looked up at me and smiled. "You were right, Mommy."

I looked up and said, "Thank you, God."

At home we found several packages stacked by our front door. We placed them under the Christmas tree. John took the baby Jesus and placed him in the manger.

Charlie built a fire, and I made hot chocolate with marshmallows. We all sat by the fireplace and drank hot chocolate from our Santa cups. The light from the fireplace cast a warm glow on the contented faces of my children. The warmth I felt wasn't from the fireplace but from my heart, which was brimming with love for my three children. I was thankful for the blessing that they always have been. I had put them through a lot, but we were all together, safe and warm.

FIFTEEN

Mr. Wonderful

I was doing an episode of "Police Woman," starring Angie Dickinson. Elinor Donahue and I were guest stars. One day while Elinor and I were waiting to go on stage, she casually asked, "Would you like to meet a friend of Harry's and mine? He's a very nice man, been divorced for a while and he's dating all the wrong kind of women."

Elinor was married to Harry Ackerman, whom I had worked for when he was producing "My Three Sons." He was a gentleman of the old school.

"Well, that might be nice. But I'll only go out with him if you and Harry go with us. That would make me feel more comfortable."

"Oh great! I'll ask him to give you a call."

Some days later I received a call from a man who said, "I hear you're riding the freedom train." I thought it was someone who thought I was working for the Civil Rights Movement.

"I beg your pardon."

"I'm Harry Ashley, and I wonder if you'd like to see "California Suite" at the Ahmanson Theater. Neil Simon's play? It's leaving next week."

I wanted to see the play, but I wasn't at all clear who this was or who had suggested that he call me.

"I saw you in that car commercial and thought you were great. Sally Powers told me she cast you." Oh, good, a clue. Later I'd call Sally to ask who Harry Ashley is. I was late for a lunch date, but I kept talking to this fellow because he was so funny. I was intrigued.

He asked if Thursday night would be OK. I was breaking all my rules about going out alone with someone I didn't know. I said, "Yes, that would be fine." Afterwards, I made a note to call Sally when I got back home… Harry Ashley?

In the restaurant I spotted a friend of mine across the room. I waved but she didn't see me. Behind her, a bearded gentleman waved back. I tried to indicate I had waved to the lady sitting in front of him. However, he stood and made his way across the room to me. Close up, he seemed familiar.

"Joyce, it's Harry Ackerman, Elinor's husband."

Oh, my goodness. I hadn't seen Harry for a year and he had grown a full beard.

"Guess you didn't recognize me with the beard. Has my friend Bill Asher telephoned you yet?"

"For heaven's sake, Harry, that's who called! He said your name and his so quickly that I put them together and thought his name was Harry Ashley!" We both laughed. I stopped and asked Harry if Bill Asher was a gentleman. Harry was very much a gentleman and I trusted him.

"Oh, yes, you'll have a lovely time, not to worry."

Thank heaven I ran into Harry. The angels were at work.

Bill called that evening. "I've been thinking you might not want to go out with me. I'm not exactly an 8-by-10 glossy. I'm no Robert Goulet. I'm bald."

I said, trying to be as silly and funny as he was, "Well, rent a wig!"

At exactly six o'clock, while I was finishing my makeup, the doorbell rang. Nine-year-old Mary rushed to the door. After a moment or two she came into the bedroom, and in a very loud voice said, "Wait 'til you see this bozo!"

Glaring at Mary, I blotted my lipstick and walked into the living room to meet Bill Asher. ... he *was* bald! But he was also the most charming, funny, intelligent man I'd ever met. We went to Musso & Frank's for dinner and talked and laughed so much that we missed the first act of the Neil Simon play.

After the performance we went backstage to see a mutual friend, Jack Weston. He gave me a big hug, then saw Bill standing behind me.

"You two together?" We nodded.

"Perfect," he said.

The next morning Bill called. "How about tonight we see the first act we missed last night, and then have dinner?" What style!

After the play I said I had to get home and to bed early because I was shooting a Saturday morning children's show, "Big John, Little John," with Herb Edelman playing my husband. (Sherwood Schwartz had promised that I would be in his next series, and he kept his promise.) Bill said, "Why don't I pick you up tomorrow morning and drive you to the studio?"

"That's five-thirty in the morning." He lived forty minutes away in Beverly Hills.

"That's OK, it'll be fun."

At five-thirty sharp he rang my doorbell. He dropped me off at the studio and rolled down the window of his green Jag. "See you at lunchtime."

"What?" I thought he was joking. I waved and went in to work.

In the middle of a scene, I looked off to the side of the set, and there I saw Bill Asher. He was watching the scene I was shooting, patiently waiting for me to break for lunch. I did get a little chill of excitement to see him. He was paying a lot of attention to me, and he was such fun to be with.

When he opened the car door for me, I noticed a picnic basket in the back seat. We drove through Hancock Park, one of my favorite neighborhoods, with old mansions and stately trees. We parked under a tree and ate our picnic lunch. I listened to more stories from this fascinating man. Bill had been married to Elizabeth Montgomery. He had produced and directed a very successful show they did together, "Bewitched." They had three children, Billy, Robert and Rebecca. Bill was unhappy about the divorce. Towards the end of the show, things started to fall apart between them, and Liz went off with the assistant director of the show. A year or so later, when that romance ended, Bill said she wanted to get back together, but he refused. He had been married to another actress before Elizabeth and had two children from that marriage, Brian and Liane.

At the end of my day of shooting, Bill asked if I would like to play tennis. He was an excellent player. Later we went to dinner and he drove me home.

Next time after work, we went to his place in Beverly Hills so I could change into my tennis clothes. He lived in a very nice house and was eager to show it to me. Above the fireplace was a portrait of a young girl. I learned later it was the young lady he had been living with. He showed me the children's rooms and told me they often came on the weekends. When I went into the dressing room to change, I found blue feathers on the floor. They looked as if they had come from a boa. This became a joke between us—I referred to any lady he had dated as "blue feathers."

The pattern of picking me up at 5:30 in the morning, driving me to the studio, having a picnic lunch under a tree in Hancock Park, and a game of tennis after work continued for a few weeks. It was fun to have such an entertaining friend. Sometimes we would go to a movie and dinner. Still, I often begged off in the evenings to be able to spend time at home with John. (Charlie was working and Mary was in Hawaii visiting Jimmy and his wife.)

One night after dinner, we were saying goodnight at my door and he said, "I hope you don't think I'm gay because I haven't made a move on you."

"No, I thought you were a gentleman. My goodness!"

He explained that he was just untangling from a relationship. A few weeks later, he asked if I would go to New York City for the Fourth of July with him. I didn't know how to ask politely, "May I have my own room?" I declined and spent that night with John, watching fireworks at the beach. When I arrived home, I saw on the doorstep a long box tied with a big red bow. In it were a dozen red roses and a card that said, "I missed you today. Bill."

When Bill returned, he came to the studio. Instead of our usual picnic, we had lunch in the commissary. Bill looked very concerned. He told me the woman he had been having a relationship with was about to have a serious operation. If she had cancer, he was going to marry her. Later that day he was flying out to be with her. What a good heart he had! But I felt sad. He said he would call to let me know the results.

Well, I never prayed so hard for someone to be well! It was then that I realized I would hate to lose this wonderful man from my life. The next day Bill called from the hospital; she would recover. All was well.

A few days later, boy and girl figures made of candy arrived at the house. The girl looked like me, and the boy like Bill. The card said, "I think we make a great couple. I hope you do too. Love, Bill."

The next day he left a gift in my dressing room, a tape deck cued up to play a song with a card that said, "Everything I feel about you is in this song." The song was "She's the One" from "A Chorus Line."

We'd only been dating a month. Bill kept saying we should get married. I told him if I said yes, he would surely run the other way. One day we drove by one of the houses I had admired when we were having our picnics. I said, "That's my favorite house. I love English-style homes." It was a beautiful stone house on a corner, overlooking a golf course, with a For Sale sign in front. Bill parked the car, looked at me and smiled.

"Would you marry me and live in this house?"

I thought of the lyrics from "Sound of Music"—somewhere in my youth or childhood, I must have done something good. I leaned over and gave Bill a kiss on his cheek.

Was I falling in love with Bill? Or was it because for the first time, I would be married to someone who would take care of me? Someone I wouldn't have to take care of? Someone who could give the children and me security? Or did I really love this man because he was so attentive, funny and kind? I didn't know.

At work, I could hardly concentrate. Bill asked me to have dinner at his new rented house and asked if I would spend the night with him. Was I ever nervous about this next step! We had such a nice relationship as friends. Maybe being intimate with him would help me know if I really loved him.

We had wine by candlelight. After dinner we went upstairs to bed and made love. In the morning when I awoke, I saw a small gift, a beautiful cameo pin. Bill brought breakfast up to bed. I was still in a fog about whether to marry him. I wanted to be certain my decision was based on love. A few weeks later, after spending more time together, and talking, talking, talking, I realized that my attraction to Bill was really love.

"Yes. Yes. I love you. I'll marry you!"

Never were two people so opposite attracted to each other like magnets.

Bill and I wanted to tell each of our children in person about our plans to be married. The very first person I told was Charlie. He had stayed home that summer from Hawaii to work at Lumber City and spend time surfing with his buddies. His reaction to the news was expected. "Mom, you've only been dating for what? Two months?" I assured him this was the right thing and told him how much I loved Bill.

Next we would tell Bill's youngest children, Billy, 11, Robert, 9, and Rebecca, 6. Bill and I had been on a few outings with them and had a great time, especially at the circus. But on this special night I wanted them to be as comfortable as possible. I was excited because I liked the children very much. But one never knows how children will respond to the idea of a stepmother. I prepared dinner for everyone at Bill's house. After dinner Bill announced with great fanfare that we were going to be married. Billy jumped out of his chair and ran around the table to hug me.

"Oh, good! We can call you Mom."

"What do you call your mother?"

"Mom."

"Well, she's very special, so why don't we think of another name for me?"

"But you're special, too."

The next night we took Liane and Brian, Bill's eldest children, from his first marriage to Dorothea Asher, to dinner at The Bat Rack in Santa Monica. This was my first meeting with Liane and Brian. They were so nice and welcoming, and seemed to take the announcement of their father's imminent marriage in stride.

With Bill's five and my three, we were going to be our own Brady Bunch! Florence Henderson had a happy, fulfilling career as Mrs. Brady. Now I, with a combined family of eight children, was about to embark on a real-life situation comedy of my own.

All the children knew, with the exception of nine-year-old Mary, who had gone to visit Jim and his wife in Hawaii. While she was in Hawaii, her stepmother had taken her for a short trip to Canada. We decided it would be nice to have a pre-honeymoon trip to Hawaii with our children. That way, we could become better acquainted as a family. When Mary came back from Canada to Hawaii, we would be able to tell her in person about our plans.

In Hawaii, five of our eight children were fast asleep in a hotel. They were being supervised by Bill's 22-year-old son, Brian. Bill and I went to the airport to greet Mary. As we waited, I stood nervously twisting the large sapphire and diamond engagement ring Bill had given me. Mary had only seen Bill ("The Bozo," as she had referred to him), a few times before she had left to see her Dad and stepmother for a month.

The day I sent Mary off for her vacation, she had her hair neatly braided in pigtails, tied with ribbons, and she wore white tights and Mary Jane shoes. That memory quickly faded when I saw my little Mary walking unsteadily down the ramp from the airplane in tight French jeans, a midriff top, lipstick, nail polish, and high lime-green wedge shoes. What happened to my sweet, demure nine-year-old? I rushed to give her a big hug and kisses. Within seconds, she grabbed my hand and spotted the ring.

"What the hell is this?"

"I'll explain everything in the car," I whispered.

Mary eyed Bill suspiciously as we walked toward the stretch limousine. She said, "Wow! We're going in this?" I got a closer look at the shoes Mary was sporting.

"So, young lady, where did you get such grown-up shoes?"

Looking at my ring, she said, "You first, Mommy."

As gently as I could, I told her that Bill was going to be her new father. Her eyes widened. "Oh, my God!" There were a few moments of silence. She looked at Bill, back at me and the ring, and repeated, "Oh, my God, oh, my God. Let me off at the next stop."

She was truly a funny little lady that night. At the hotel we took her to the bar for a Coca-Cola. Bill and I must have had something stronger. The next bit of news was that she had three new brothers and a sister asleep upstairs. Liane, Bill's eldest daughter, I explained, wasn't able to come with us on the trip, and Charlie had stayed home to work. So she would meet only four of the new family. Another moment of silence, then Mary's blue eyes widened again.

"Oh, my God."

I took this shocked, tired and staggering little girl upstairs. In the living room her first new brother was asleep on a sofa bed, the sheet up around his face. Gently I lowered the sheet to reveal red-bearded Brian, in his early twenties.

"Oh, my God."

Then we led her into a bedroom where two new brothers, Billy and Robert, were sleeping. Billy was eleven and Robert was nine. Mary looked closely at their sleeping faces. A smile spread slowly across her face.

"Oh, my God. They're cute." She followed us to the room where four- and five-year-old John and Rebecca were sleeping. I moved the sheet down from John's face.

"That one looks like John."

"It is, honey."

She tiptoed around the side of the bed to look at Rebecca, whose blonde hair was tousled about her face.

John and Rebecca

"Oh, my, she's so sweet."

We left the room and quietly closed the door. Mary leaned against the door, looked up at us and said one final "Oh, my God."

On August 28, all the children were part of our wedding ceremony in the chapel at All Saints Episcopal Church in Beverly Hills. Our wedding guests couldn't tell which of the younger children belonged to Elizabeth Montgomery and which were mine; they all looked like one family. Rebecca and John looked like twins!

At the reception when I took Rebecca, age six, into the ladies room with me, I kneeled down to give her a big hug. She said, "Mommy wanted me to tell you she hopes you'll be very happy." I always said Bill's children were mine from the heart. I love them all very much and thank their mothers for sharing them with me.

Bill had an incredible honeymoon planned for us, a trip on a Concorde jet to Paris and an elegant stay in a hotel in Monte Carlo. But first we were going to have four days at the Beach Club in Laguna.

When I opened the door to our honeymoon suite, I saw flowers with a card: "To Mrs. William Asher, You are like an angel from heaven who has been sent to me." I couldn't help but think about another night in Laguna many years ago with Roger. He was now married to JoAnne Worley. I hoped he was as happy as I was.

Wedding Day; so happy

Before we left for Laguna, I had arranged for Mary's tenth birthday party. We would be back in time to help her celebrate. It was very important to be there; it just wouldn't do to have her mother get married and then abandon her on her birthday.

I had had many long talks with Bill about the importance of my children in my life. I told him, "Because my children were in my life before you, they are my first responsibility. If you can understand that, I can marry you. If not, it just won't work."

The day we were supposed to leave The Beach Club, I was packing my suitcase when Bill came in and asked, "What are you doing?"

"I'm just getting packed. What time do you want to leave?"

"Are you kidding? You don't really think we're going home?"

I was speechless. When I found my voice I said, "We have to be home for Mary's birthday."

"I thought you were kidding about that."

"Oh, no. It would be awful not be there for her party."

"I don't believe you!" He gave me a disapproving look and left the room. We sat in silence all the way back.

While I was overseeing the décor of our new home, we were living in my little house. Everything was mostly under control so that we could leave on our big honeymoon trip. I was over the moon with excitement. My bags were all packed with beautiful new clothes. We were leaving in a day and a half, and I was counting every minute. Bill came home late from the studio said he had already eaten. He poured a drink and came in the bedroom to talk to me while I busied myself with last-minute things for the trip.

He took a long sip of his drink.

"I don't think I should leave the show and go on the trip. They need me there."

I stopped what I was doing, "But you've paid for the tickets and everything is planned."

"Yeah, well I can't help it."

"I thought you were just a consultant. They knew you were going on your honeymoon." Tears formed in my eyes.

"That's just the way it is. Sorry."

My own "Brady Bunch"

SIXTEEN

Home Sweet Home— Where Is It?

Our first home was the beautiful English home in Hancock Park that I loved so much. Bill had purchased my dream home and said, "Everything I have is yours." I had sold my home and used all the money from that sale to decorate this most magnificent home on the Wilshire Country Club Golf Course.

On moving day Bill went to work at the studio. I had four bedrooms of furniture coming in two large vans, and Bill had five bedrooms of furniture arriving on large flatbeds in crates that had been in storage while he rented a house. It looked as if the circus had arrived in town. The vans and flatbeds filled the entire block. I stood in front of our new home directing the movers where to place each piece of furniture in the house.

It seemed from the houses that Bill had rented and furnished, that we had similar taste, English Country. Inside, our home was filled with a combination of English antiques and country furniture. But

Beautiful on the outside, sad on the inside

emerging from storage were some very strange pieces; an oversized carved gold headboard, a large lacquered chest inlaid with dragons, black lacquered coffee tables, orange lacquered end tables. I asked the movers to set those pieces aside in the driveway. Soon there were more orange, red, black and gold pieces than the driveway could hold. After the movers left, I looked at the pile of furniture in the driveway. There was much too much furniture, and not my taste at all. Bill and I had only known each other three months before we heard, "Here Comes the Bride." During that time he never mentioned any fondness for Chinese furniture. What was I to do with this pile in the driveway? Bill had left the movers to me and told me to arrange everything just as I wanted it in our house. I called my experienced friend Betty Bullock, known by all her friends as "Mouth of brass, Heart of gold." Betty said, "Don't worry, I'll be right over."

She eyed the pile of furniture in the driveway as critically as I had.

"This will never fit in your house, and it's ugly as hell. We'll call A-Bell Auctioneers and they'll take it off your hands."

"Betty, how can I sell Bill's furniture?"

"First of all, it won't fit in the house. And it's as ugly as sin. He told you to do what you want, right?"

"Right." An A-Bell Auctioneer arrived and offered $500 for the whole pile.

"Great, she'll take it," Betty said.

"Oh, Betty, I can't. I'm sure that God-awful headboard alone is worth five times more than they're offering."

"Did he tell you to do what you want, or not? Did he leave you in charge, or not?"

"I know, I know." I hesitated, wanting to get rid of the pile, afraid Bill might say I had to live with it.

"No, I can't, I just can't."

I thanked the man and Betty for their trouble. They both left in a huff. At my request the gardener got a tarp to cover the pile so the damp night air wouldn't ruin the furniture.

I continued unpacking the books in the library while I waited for Bill to come home. The amount of impressive work that my new husband had done amazed me. I dusted and placed leather-bound scripts of shows Bill had directed: I Love Lucy, The Flying Nun, The Shirley Temple Storybook Show, Our Miss Brooks, The Danny Thomas Show, The Patty Duke Show, The Dinah Shore Chevy Show, scripts of all the Beach Party movies he wrote and directed, all the Bewitched scripts. With reverence and awe, I leafed through the script of the Kennedy Inauguration Gala, which he had directed and Frank Sinatra produced. I knew he was a wonderful man, but I had no idea how brilliant his career had been. In a moment I would have to greet him at our front door, this brilliant man I married, and explain how his furniture didn't fit in with our English antiques.

Bill arrived home after dark. I felt like genuflecting. Such a list of credits, the likes of which I'd never seen. Not once had he mentioned his accomplishments during our brief courtship. He gave me a kiss and said, "Honey, what's that big pile in the driveway under the tarp?"

"Well, all the furniture wouldn't fit in the house, so I covered it so it wouldn't get wet."

"Oh, I see. What wouldn't fit?" He walked out toward the pile. I followed a few steps behind. He lifted the tarp; I held my breath.

"Where did this come from?"

"It was your furniture you had in storage."

"Honey, this isn't mine. It's what I took out of the house I was renting. It was so ugly I replaced it with my own furniture. It belongs to the people I rented the house from. They must have moved it here by mistake."

"Oh, no! I almost sold all their furniture this afternoon to the auctioneers. Thank God I didn't, and thank God you didn't like it! I love you!"

School started. John and Mary were off in the mornings to a private school in the valley, and Charlie was in high school at The Harvard School. On the weekends and holidays, Bill's three youngest children came to stay with us. Our children adjusted to each other more easily than we did. It was a strained and difficult time. Our differences involved our children and our lack of time alone together.

For Halloween, I decorated the breakfast room with cobwebs, witches and pumpkins. Bats hung from the ceiling. Billy, Robert and Rebecca's nanny brought the children over for trick or treating. I showed them the Halloween room and took them upstairs to surprise their Dad. They were all in costume, with painted faces.

Bill was resting. They stood by the bed and shouted, "Trick or Treat!"

"What the hell are they doing here?"

I was shocked. I ushered the children out of the room.

"He was just sleepy. He didn't mean it."

We went to trick or treat in the neighborhood. The children were running up and down and having great fun. I faked it. How could Bill react to his children like that? When Liz and Bill were married and both working, their household was run differently. The children had their playroom and their own dining room and bedrooms, but the rest of the house was for adults only, except on Christmas, when a decorator did the house. I wanted our home to have fewer boundaries for our children.

It was Christmas time. Oh, what a beautiful house for me and the children to decorate, like the most beautiful Christmas card! Unaware that Bill didn't care for Christmas, I asked him if we could go get our Christmas tree together.

"What do you mean? The florist will bring a tree and decorate the house."

"Oh, no. We like to decorate it ourselves. It's much more fun. I'll go to the flower mart and buy garlands for the staircase and over the doorways."

"You know how to do all that?"

"Oh, yes. I love doing it." Begrudgingly, he agreed we would get a tree.

"I'll get the children all bundled up." I shouted up the staircase, "Charlie, Mary, John! Get your coats and scarves. We're going to get our Christmas tree!"

Bill frowned. "They're not coming, are they?"

"Of course, we'll have so much fun! Every year we go to the valley and find a Christmas tree lot where they have an outdoor fire and hot chocolate for everyone. Then we all run around looking for the prettiest tree. You've never done that?"

"No."

"You'll have fun, I promise." (I wasn't so sure.)

The children jumped in the car. Bill drove about five blocks to Wilshire Boulevard and stopped at the first Christmas tree lot. He got out and pointed to a large tree. We heard him tell the man to deliver it. He gave the address and got back in the car. Silence all the way home.

In November, right before Thanksgiving, Bill had given me piles of papers to sign, quitclaim deeds on everything he owned, including our new home. (Earlier he said that the house would be ours together.) He said his business manager drew up the papers. I was dumbstruck. I had put all my money into our new home, which now would be his alone. I had sold my car because Bill wanted me to drive his Cadillac, while he would drive his Jag. The cars were in his name, of course. All of a sudden I had nothing.

What if Bill wanted to leave me? With three children to take care of, I panicked at the thought of being destitute. I signed the papers, even though I didn't have to, because I wanted Bill to know I married him for love, not money. But had I known that I would have nothing, I would have kept my money from the sale of my home separately.

When Bill worked late, I would keep his dinner and reheat it for him. No matter how late it was, he had his routine. He would wake me, shower, put on a cashmere sweater and his velvet slippers, then join me in the library where he had his two vodkas. I sat with him while he had his dinner on a tray.

On one of these late nights he said, "Everything I thought I wanted, I don't want."

"What?"

"Remember when I told you that I used to drive by houses at night and see the lights on, and families gathered around together?"

"Yes," I said hesitantly.

"It's just what I *thought* I wanted, but I don't."

"I don't understand?" If this was true, maybe I could just die and I wouldn't hurt so much. What had I done? He didn't like our life? It wasn't what he wanted? I suddenly felt as if my body had been twisted, squeezed and wrung out like an old mop. My dream of a happy marriage had turned out to be just that, a dream. It was like one of those fake houses on the back lot of a studio, beautiful on the outside, but a facade held up with wood stakes that can be kicked out from under. Then the house falls down.

My children. Oh, God, my children!

I went upstairs and fell on our bed like a heavy sack. Bill wanted to make love almost every night of our marriage. It was wonderful to feel desired, but not tonight.

The next morning I went into my beautiful marble bathroom to take a shower. I sobbed so hard my body shook uncontrollably. I slid down the corner of the shower and thought the only way to end this pain was to end my life. Then the thought of my children and how they needed me pulled me out of the darkest, most desperate place I had ever been. I picked myself up off the floor and started to make a plan. That evening I told Bill that since he was so unhappy with our life, it would be best for us to end our marriage. With as much strength as I could muster, I said, "I don't want anything. I just want what I had when I came into this marriage. I put all my money into this house and everything else into the hands of your business manager. I just want to be back where I was before we married. I would like a home like the one I sold, with a bedroom for each child and a swimming pool."

He said he would move to a hotel and we would look for a house for the children and me. In the six months since our marriage, real estate had gone sky high. When Bill came to pick me up to go house-hunting, we were stiff and uncomfortable together. The weather was warm outside, but inside the car it was frigid. I was stoic and resolute. Bill drove me to the worst part of the valley and pointed out a pea green house near the freeway. He thought this would work for the children and me. Hurt and insulted, I said I would look on my own. It was impossible to find anything as charming as my previous home. Eventually I found a small Spanish-style house on a hill in the valley. It didn't have a swimming pool, but it seemed peaceful, with a view of a lake through the trees. It cost a bit more than my old home, but the market had taken such a huge leap that this seemed fair. The English house sold very quickly, for a profit, and was in escrow. The children and I would be living in it until escrow closed.

I was offered a leading role in the Detroit Company of "Vanities." Rehearsals would be in Los Angeles, and there was a limited run scheduled for Detroit. I wouldn't have to be away from the children very long, and they could come to see me during school vacation. I needed to start making money!

When I arrived in Detroit, bouquets of flowers arrived every day from Bill. I put them in the hallway—I didn't want anything from him. Most of the time I was upset and sad, feeling I was doing terrible harm to my children by my marriages and the constant moving from place to place.

In the suburbs of Detroit, I rented a house with one of the other actresses in the play. It was spring. Lilies of the valley lined the paths in a nearby wood and the scent of lilacs filled the air. I took long walks in the afternoon before going to the theater, and I read books about marriage and relationships. I took every test in the self-help books, trying to learn what made a successful relationship.

Bill surprised me on Mother's Day. He arrived in my dressing room with my three children. Oh, was I ever happy to see them! And Bill too. His usually twinkly eyes looked sad. He asked if he could stay for a few days so we could talk. We spent hours walking through the woods, sitting by the lake and talking about our marriage. I told him about the books I had read, which helped with communication. I said, "I can give and give until I break, but I don't want to break, and I don't want you to break either." We both wanted our marriage to work, so we each gave. We bent like two willows toward each other so neither of us had to break.

Bill surprised me when he said he had never liked the English house in Hancock Park. He had been building a house in Benedict Canyon that he preferred. But the rooms for the children looked out on a cement retaining wall, like little cells. I suggested we build a wing onto his house in the canyon, with an upstairs to give the children sunshine and trees outside their windows. Although I was concerned that living in Benedict Canyon wasn't a great place for the children—there wasn't a neighborhood with friends to play with—we were each bending. He would live in the house that made him happy, and we would build a wing for the children, and that would make me happy.

My biggest concern was the large hill behind the concrete retaining wall. I worried that it could someday give way to a mudslide. We built the new wing on the canyon house and started rebuilding our relationship. Bill's son, Billy, and his snake came to live with us and soon Robert followed. Liz thought it was best to have Rebecca live with her and come to us on weekends and holidays. We had a very big family now, and it was lots of fun. Bill started to enjoy being a father.

Thanksgiving; feeling so blessed

The children and I were giving him so much love and attention, he couldn't resist.

However, he never ate dinner with the children and me. He would bring his two drinks to the table and drink while we talked about the events of the day over our dinner. When we finished, he had his dinner. I didn't like it, but I was bending.

One night when Bill and I were in bed reading and waiting for Mary to come home from dinner with Jim, she came running upstairs to our bedroom and sobbing, threw herself into my arms.

"Oh honey, what's wrong? What's the matter?"

Through her sobs I barely made out her answer, "Daddy."

"Your Daddy? Honey, I can't understand, I can't understand you." Her face was buried in my arms and through the sobs I heard, "Daddy, Daddy."

"Honey, is your Daddy all right?"

More sobs. "Daddy is so mean."

"Oh honey, what happened?"

"He's just so mean to me." I had been afraid that Mary, now ten, would be the brunt of his cruelty. I didn't know what to say. I dried her tears. Bill reached over, stroked her hair and gave her a kiss. I took her upstairs to her room, helped her get undressed and tucked her into bed. I tried to explain.

"Honey, it isn't your fault. I think what makes your Daddy mean sometimes is that he was adopted. He felt abandoned by his mother. Then Grammy was always away and he was left with a nanny. That was another feeling of abandonment. Then his sister, Mary, the one you're named after, died. He was very close to her. When Mommy divorced him, he felt abandoned again. It isn't you. Please know your Daddy loves you very much. All right? And Bill and I love you so much. Now, sweet one, try to go to sleep and know how much you are loved."

I turned the lights off and said, "Don't forget your prayers."

So many times, when Jim had been cruel to me when we were eating in restaurants, I fled to the ladies' room in tears. My poor little Mary! How could I help make her strong enough not to be hurt by her father?

One of the most frightening nights I've ever experienced as a mother happened the first year of my marriage to Bill. We had taken the kids to an early Sunday movie, all except John and Charlie. Charlie, now 17, stayed home to do his homework and be there when Ed brought John, now five, home. This was one of John's infrequent visits with his father. I had asked Ed to bring John home by 7:30 because he had school the next day.

When we arrived home at 8:30, Charlie was standing at the front door with a frightened look. Right away my mind raced. "Charlie, where's John? What's wrong?"

Charlie took me by the arm and walked me out of earshot of Robert, Billy and Mary.

I started to panic. "What is it, Charlie? Honey, please tell me. Is John OK?"

"Mom, Ed's friend is downstairs. He came over to tell you that he's scared for John. Ed's drunk out of his mind and has John locked in a closet. He's been throwing things at John and he wouldn't let his friend bring John home."

"Oh God, Charlie." I tried to be calm, but my heart was racing. I started for the phone. Thinking out loud, I said, "I'm going to call Ed's doctor and ask him what to do. I don't want him to hurt John." I searched for the number of the psychiatrist Ed had been seeing. Fingers shaking, I dialed. There was an emergency number on the answering machine. I dialed it.

"Doctor, this is Joyce Asher. I was married to your patient, Ed Mallory." I explained the situation. He said he would call Ed and call me right back. I hung up and paced the floor. He didn't call back, and each minute seemed like an eternity. What was happening to my little boy? I couldn't stand another minute of the panic and fear surging through my body, as if someone had reached deep down inside me and was taking my insides out very slowly.

Bill was trying to calm me.

"Oh, honey," I said to Bill, "let's go to Ed's house so that when the doctor tells us what to do, we'll be right there." Charlie wanted to go too. We asked Ed's friend to tell the doctor we would call back in a few minutes. It was a half-hour drive over the hill. I was trying hard to be calm, but I was terrified for John. Bill drove and Charlie held my hand as I willed the car to go faster and faster. I said a prayer over and over.

"Please protect John, please don't let John be hurt, dear God I beg you, don't let John be hurt."

Ed's friend told us that Ed was half naked and had cut his feet on glass and dishes he was throwing. He had been running in the yard and screaming. His friend begged us not to tell Ed that he had let us know what was going on.

Oh God! I was so frightened for John. Finally, the phone booth was in sight. I leaped out of the car and called the doctor's emergency number.

"This is Joyce Asher. What should we do, Doctor?"

"Ed is very drunk. I told him I was calling you to tell you that he is sick and that you would get John. Now, whatever you do, do not go into the house alone. Can someone go with you?"

"Yes, my husband and son are with me."

"Take your son. Do not take Bill—he's very angry about your marriage to Bill."

"I have Charlie with me."

"That's good. I told Ed to have John at the front door, ready to go."

"Thank you, doctor. I'm leaving right now." I knew Ed had a gun.

I got into the car with Charlie next to me. As we reached the top of the hill at Ed's house, we saw two police cars with flashing red lights. No lights were on in the house. I stopped the car in the middle of the road and ran out. I was afraid if Ed saw the police, he might get angry and hurt John. I ran to the police in the front yard.

"My little boy is in there, and I'm afraid for him. Please go around the corner out of sight. Just wait in case I need you." I ran to the front door and rang the doorbell. No answer. I rang again. By then Charlie was by my side. I heard a plaintive voice say, "Mommy! Mommy!"

"Yes, John, honey, it's Mommy. Open the door."

"I can't. It won't open."

"Try again, honey, you can open it."

"No, I can't." He started crying.

"It's OK, honey, it's OK."

"Mommy, I can't."

"John, go to the kitchen door and try that." Charlie and I ran around the side of the house to the kitchen door. Curtains blocked our view through the glass pane door. His little voice again cried, "Mommy, I can't open the door."

"It's OK, honey, it's OK." I tried to sound reassuring. "Try again, you can do it!"

I said to Charlie, "We'll break the glass if we have to." Just then, the door opened and there stood John with his tear-streaked face. I picked him up and hugged him with all my might.

"Thank you, God, thank you."

As we left, I told the police that I had my little boy, but they should check on the man inside. I had been told he was drunk and bleeding. Ed could bleed to death for all I cared.

Because of Ed's behavior, John was too frightened to see him. I felt sorrow and empathy for Ed, but I never wanted my son to be placed in jeopardy again. It was necessary to go to court so what had happened would be on record. If anything else occurred, I would have the right to discontinue visitations. Going to court was the best way for me to protect John. The judge decided Ed couldn't drink twenty-four hours before or during a visit with John. For a long time, when John was too frightened to see his father, Ed thought I was influencing John not to see him. But I was doing just the opposite. I was trying to make John feel comfortable about seeing his father… but how could he? Bill wanted to adopt John, but Ed would not permit it.

*

That spring I went to Kansas City to star in a production of "A Girl Could Get Lucky." The director became ill during rehearsals. Bill had been visiting me in Kansas, and just as he was boarding a plane to return home, I had him paged. "Honey, you have to come back!"

I could barely hear his voice over the noise at the airport.

"I'll be back soon, I'll miss you. I love you."

"No, wait! Honey, I need you to come back and direct the play!"

"What? What did you say?"

I yelled into the phone, "Direct the play. The director is ill."

"I've never directed a play."

"Yes you have! It's just like directing 'I love Lucy.' Please, you'll be great." He was great, and the play was a huge success.

The builder I had worked for, after Ed and I divorced, called and asked to meet with me. I invited him over. In the living room with Bill and me, he spread out a blueprint on the coffee table.

"I'm doing very well with several developments. Thanks to you, they are mostly English country homes. I'd like you to come work for me. You would have your own office, where you would help the buyers pick out their finishes, the fixtures, flooring, lighting, and carpeting. You would also be able to act as their decorator, if you want, and you could still have your own personal clients. I'm offering you $100,000!"

I looked at Bill. He said, "Joyce is an actress and I would advise her not to do this."

I jumped in. "Why don't I give you a call after we talk it over."

He folded up his blueprints. I thanked him for the offer and said I would call in a day or two. After he left, I said to Bill, "I would really like to do this. I could make a great deal of money, especially since he said I would be able to run my own decorating business from my office."

Very sternly, Bill said, "You are an actress, you need to act!"

"But, honey, I don't have any money. The money I make doing shows goes to your business manager, and everything is in your name. I would feel much more secure if I could have my own business. I like doing interior design."

"Would you feel more secure if we had the house in both of our names?"

"Yes, of course I would."

"If I put the house in both our names, I would like you to keep acting and not take this job." I wondered, is this another bending moment, a compromise?

"If you really don't want me to take the job..."

He looked at me with a big smile. "You're an actress."

I didn't take the job. Our home and every home we purchased after that was in both our names. Bill made certain that I kept acting. He wanted me to do a series that he would direct. When he directed the series "Bad News Bears" that Jack Warden stared in, I played Jack's love interest.

At first, I wasn't at all interested in being in the film "Airplane." It was the silliest script I'd ever read. But Bill said, "You're an actress..act!" The film was named one of the funniest hundred movies ever made. Then I was a guest on the series "Alice," which led to a starring role on a spin-off of that show, "The Flo Show" and the famous line, "Kiss my Grits!" Bill directed "Charley's Aunt" for HBO, and I played opposite Charles Grodin.

In the fall, our home was a little less lively because Charlie was away at college. One rainy Sunday afternoon, Bill and I and our friend Jack Warden decided to go see our new home, which was being remodeled.

Bill and I had decided it would be better and more convenient for the children to live in a neighborhood, instead of the canyon, which had proved difficult for them. Billy and Mary stayed home to do homework, and John was visiting a friend. The rain was coming down, not in drops, but in sheets. We were in the car, and the canyon was filling with rainwater. When we tried to get to our new house, the streets were flooded and there was no way to reach the driveway. Jack scoffed, "So, you've already bought this place? Too late to back out?" We gave a hollow laugh and explained that the house we were in now was closing escrow in three days, and the new owners were excited to be moving in.

On the way, we dropped in on our friends, A.J. and Caryl. Their beautiful home in Brentwood looked like a disaster had hit; pots and pans were catching water, and towels were stuffed on the window sills to stop torrents of rain from coming in. Caryl offered us tea. We bemoaned the rainstorm that hadn't let up for days. When I finished my tea, I looked at my watch, noticed it was four o'clock, and decided to call home. Uneasy about the rain, I wanted to check on Mary and Billy. Bill called me a worrywart, but something told me to call. I got a busy signal. I waited and called again. Still busy, three more times.

"Bill, I can't get through on the phone."

"Everything's OK, the kids are probably gabbing."

We thanked the Carothers, and the three of us ran through the pouring rain to the car. I wanted to go home, so we dropped Jack off and started driving up Benedict Canyon. As we rounded a corner, debris came rushing down toward us like a river. Large tree branches, patio furniture, outdoor umbrellas, garbage cans. The car in front of us started floating backward in our direction. The driver waved to us to go back. We couldn't get home!

"Honey, let's go to the Beverly Hills Hotel and try to call the children again." Bill thought I was overreacting, but seeing my alarm, he pulled up to the big pink hotel. The lobby had buckets of water all around. Women in evening gowns were trying to dodge the dripping water. I ran to the phone booth and got the busy signal. Butterflies took up residence in my stomach. I called our next door neighbor, Sally Hanson.

"Hi Sally, it's Joyce. I can't reach the children. Is everything OK up there?"

"Let me put David on with you." A lifetime passed until David came on.

"Joyce, your house has been wrecked. The hill behind it gave way and crashed right through the retaining wall. Mary and Billy are with us. They're OK, just shook up."

"Oh, no! Tell them we'll get up there right away."

"You can't come up. The police have barricaded the canyons because they're like rivers. They're completely closed off."

"We'll find a way. Tell the kids we're on our way." I hung up and looked at Bill.

"The kids are OK, but the retaining wall gave way and the house has been badly damaged. Thank God they're not hurt!"

We went around to Coldwater Canyon. I got out and moved the barricades to the side so we could drive through. It was dark. We could hardly see our way, but we continued up Coldwater Canyon, which was flooded. Water and debris barreled down but Bill managed to dodge everything that came at us. When we reached Mulholland Drive at the top of the canyon, we could hear mud sliding off the hills. Bill skillfully avoided huge piles of mud and rocks.

The rain had let up a bit. We put the windows down in order to see. You could hear rocks falling and mud slushing down from the hills. At last we reached our driveway. We scrambled up the steps to our front door. Through the windows we could see showerheads sticking out into the hallway, headboards pushed right through the wall. The mudslide had lifted up the bottom of the house and flowed through the bedrooms and family room. And the stairs leading up to the children's room had collapsed. Charlie's room was filled with mud and the headboard was crushed. If he had been asleep when this happened, he would have been killed. I started crying and Bill, trying to lighten things up, said, "It looks just like it does when he's home."

We got in the car and drove up the hill to Sally's. It had started raining again. Sally met us with an umbrella, a warm hug, and a tall vodka.

"I hope you don't mind; Mary and Billy were so shaken that I gave them a shot of brandy."

They came running for hugs the minute we opened the door. Billy and Mary were so smart! Billy had turned off the gas, and Mary had called a local radio announcer who was reporting road conditions. On the radio she had said, "If my Mom is listening, our house was damaged but Billy and I are OK." Billy had put a note on the door telling us where they were. We found it several days later, floating in the rainwater.

Helen was visiting in Los Angeles, staying with her friend, Laura Mako. They heard Mary on the radio and called the station. Someone at the station called Mary.

"Some crazy lady claiming to be Helen Hayes called. She says she's your grandmother."

"That *is* my grandmother!"

"In that case, we're going to put you on the air, live."

"Miss Hayes, there's your granddaughter on the line."

"Oh, Mary, darling, so glad you're safe! But you're late for dinner! I'm here with Nancy Sinatra, Jacques Mapes and Ross Hunter. We're having a wonderful spaghetti dinner, had to start without you, dear. Glad you're OK. Bye, dear."

The next day when we went to our wreck of a house, I saw that the clocks had stopped at four o'clock, exactly the time I had felt the need to call. When the people who wanted to buy our house came for a final inspection, were they ever surprised! Their dream house had gone from six bedrooms to three. They canceled the escrow.

We went to work on extensive repairs, which took months. In the meantime we moved into our new home in Brentwood, a wonderful modern house in an avocado grove, and a tree in the living room that went right through the roof.

While I was about to do a run-through of "The Flo Show" for the network, I got an emergency call. Our housekeeper, driving John to his tutor, was hit sideways. The passenger side John was sitting on was smashed in. They were not hurt, just very shaken. This was when I hated acting, when one of children needed me. Even though I was assured everyone was all right, I still wanted to rush to them, but I couldn't.

When I got home, I hugged John close.

"Look, Mommy, remember the shiny new penny you gave me? Well, I dropped it and was reaching for it when the other car hit us. If I hadn't

With John

moved when I was reaching for the penny, my leg would have been smashed. It really is a lucky penny!"

*

Summer was around the corner when I was asked to play Molly Brown in "The Unsinkable Molly Brown" in Kansas City. I was thrilled! As a young actress at the American Academy of Dramatic Arts in New York, unable to afford a ticket except for standing room, I stood in the back of the theater watching Tammy Grimes play Molly. She was so full of spit and vinegar in that role! But I think the reason it appealed to me so much was that she was a tomboy, and she had a song, "I Ain't Down Yet," with the line "I'm Gonna Learn to Read and Write." Well, I had had trouble learning to read and write, and the way she sang it, I identified 100% with the song.

> "I'm gonna learn to read and write,
> I'm gonna see what there is to see,
> So if you go from nowhere
> On the road to somewhere
> And you meet anyone
> You'll know it's me."

Molly Brown went on to be the Queen of Denver. She was flamboyant, she was honest, not the least bit pretentious—she said snails taste like erasers (I agree with her; it's the garlic that makes them good). I identified with Molly; she was a survivor, a survivor on the Titanic! I said, "Someday, someday, I'm going to do that role! I have to do that role!"

I had the best time of my life as Molly Brown. When I sang that song, I had so much invested in the song and in that character. That

"The Unsinkable Molly Brown"

role was my favorite performance of all. Even to the point that one day I toured Molly Brown's house in Denver. When I listened to the docent, I felt as if I had died and come back and was listening to someone talk about my life. A couple of times I wanted to say, no, no, it wasn't that way! That's how much I identified with her character.

With school out, Mary and John were able to go to Kansas with me. Mary was cast as the little French maid, and John was the newspaper boy who danced and sang in one number. The producers rented a big old house for us. Once a week I invited the entire cast over for a swim and snacks. We all became good friends.

Charlie was coming to town for his birthday. I thought it would be fun to surprise him with a visit from my Daddy, his grandfather, whom he had never met. My stepsister, Janet, lived in Kansas City. I felt shy about calling her, but I asked if Daddy and his wife Jackie could stay with her. The night of Charlie's birthday, at the end of the play, I had a cake brought out and the audience sang "Happy Birthday." Then Daddy came on stage.

I said, "Charlie, I'd like you to meet your Granddaddy." They exchanged big hugs and of course I cried. The next night we were all invited to dinner at Janet's home. Daddy sat at the head and regaled us with funny stories. Then he told one that broke my heart.

"Charlie, I remember when I read in the newspaper that your Mommy was going to marry your Daddy. Oh, it was big news in the papers. 'James MacArthur, son of Helen Hayes, to marry Joyce Bulifant.' Well, I went down to the hull of my boat, The Bonita, and dusted off my old tuxedo. I hung it out in the salt air to freshen it up and waited for your Mommy to call. I knew she'd ask me to give her away, but the call never came. I guess it's just as well. I had nothing but a pair of old tennis shoes to wear with my tuxedo."

I reached over and gave my Daddy's rough hands a gentle squeeze. I had no idea. Charles, whom I called Dad, had walked me down the aisle. I ached to think of Daddy, sitting on his boat with his tuxedo, waiting for the call that never came.

SEVENTEEN

Not the Perfect Mother

One Christmas, Bill and I took the family to Snowmass, Colorado, where Charlie was a ski instructor during his winter break. My mother, "Fifi" to her grandchildren, came along, and a friend of Rebecca's, Jessica Hancock, the daughter of Herbie and Gigi, were also part of our group. This was going to be a picture-perfect, old-fashioned Christmas.

I asked the realtors to find us a big log cabin where we could roast marshmallows, put our feet up, and relax while we watched the flames dance in the fireplace. When I opened the door to the "cabin," the place resembled the Guggenheim Museum. There was a modern fireplace, white walls, white furniture, and highly polished wooden floors. Not a place you want to bring a group of rowdy youngsters!

They had to be reminded to take off boots, wet ski clothes and gloves before even thinking about entering the house. Every night I cooked for about 14 people, including stray ski instructors that Charlie brought home. While everyone was out skiing, I was grocery shopping. By the time dinner was on the table, I was ready for bed. But I still clung to my dream of a perfect old-fashioned Christmas.

I sent the older children to the woods with an ax to chop down a Christmas tree. Then I put out colored paper, scissors, crayons and glitter for the younger ones to make decorations. Rebecca and Jessica helped bake cookies and cakes, and I decorated the long dining table with pinecones and berries. Of course, I had pictured all of this in a log cabin. But we were all together and it was Christmas Eve.

We piled into two cars and drove to the community church for midnight service. As we entered the church, I spotted a little red dog sitting in the snow and I leaned over to pet him. He started a low, menacing growl so I decided to leave him alone.

In church there was no room for us all to sit together. John ended up sitting in a pew on the aisle next to a fashionable Aspen lady in a fur coat. During the singing of "Silent Night," everyone lit their candles. I kept an eye on John who was having difficulty holding his candle upright. Due to the late hour, he started to doze off, and his candle got dangerously close to the lady in the fur coat. As we exited the church, snow was falling. The sound of church bells and people singing as they carried their candles out into gently falling snow was the picture-perfect Christmas I had imagined. I saw the little red dog waiting patiently in the snow for his master. I had one arm around Rebecca and I held John's hand as we walked toward the car. All of a sudden there was a loud growling sound behind us and a not-so-reverent "Jesus Christ!" Startled, I looked back and, to my horror, Bill's hand was being torn apart by the little red dog he had stopped to pet. He wrestled his hand free and walked toward us, blood dripping onto the freshly fallen snow.

Back in our Guggenheim Museum, as I bandaged Bill's hand, I said to the tired group, "There's an early Christmas gift on your beds.

Please unwrap your gift, put it on and come back upstairs. We can hold hands around our little tree."

There was a joint protest. "Can't we do that in the morning?" I had bought matching nightgowns for the girls and my mother, and red long johns for the boys, including Bill. And I insisted they put them on. "OK, everyone, come and gather around our little tree." Groans and moans came from the bedrooms.

"Go to sleep, Mom."

"Good night, Mom, see you in the morning."

"I can make hot chocolate for everyone!"

"Mom, GO to SLEEP!"

"I love you. Merry Christmas."

I looked at our old-fashioned tree and smiled at my silliness.

Bill and Elizabeth were the kind of parents who put their heads in the sand when problems with the children came up. One night while all the children were still living at home, Bill and I had gone to dinner and I desperately needed to talk with him about one of the children. He looked at me and asked, "Are you going to ruin our whole evening?"

The children's well-being was left in my hands, and it felt like a very big responsibility. Their troubled teen years, plus John's struggle with dyslexia, became overwhelming. Bill and I were going to New York and I needed to arrange all the children's activities before we left. We were in a restaurant in Westwood. I was drinking a glass of red wine and Bill was having his usual vodka.

I hesitantly asked, "When do you think we'll be back from New York?"

"Why do you keep asking? Why? I told you I would tell you when I know. Why do you have to know?"

All of a sudden his voice became fainter and seemed to come from within a tunnel. I looked at the wine glass in my hand. If I broke the glass and cut my hand, it would be painful, but not as painful as the sound of "Why do you have to know? Why do you keep asking me?" A primal scream came from the very bottom of my being right through my body. I thought I must be mad. I slumped back in the booth, weak and faint, as if I might pass out. They'll take me to the hospital and take care of me. Everything will be all right. I'll just wait here for the ambulance. Why aren't they coming? I need someone to help me. I could faintly hear talk between Bill and someone, a doctor? When would they come? Oh please, I need help.

Bill's holding on to me, helping me up, walking me through the restaurant. Out in the air, I feel a little stronger. We walk to the car. Bill helps me in and closes the door.

The incident was never mentioned.

A great deal of my focus was on John, who was having a hard time in a special school for dyslexic children. His eleventh birthday was coming up.

"John, honey, what would you like to do for your birthday?"

"I don't want a party."

"Why not?"

"Because when I was ten everybody said, 'You're ten and you don't know that?' Now they're just going to say, 'You're eleven and you don't know that?' I don't want to be eleven."

I put my arm around him. "You'll be just fine. You're learning a lot."

So much attention was focused on John's difficulties in school that Mary, now fifteen, was getting lost in the shuffle. She was having great difficulty in school and going through a rebellious time. She wasn't too happy with the strict rules at home. Mary was able to convince her father, Jimmy, and Grammy Helen that she should go to board-ing school. She chose a school that had few guidelines or rules. I was concerned, but headstrong Miss Mary packed up her belongings and headed to boarding school. I hoped she would be happy, but I knew her secret reason for wanting to go was to get away from Mom's rules. She had a grand time at boarding school—party! party! party!

Often she called sick from the infirmary and I, the Worrywart Mom, asked the school to get her a counselor to help her through this rebellious period. From so far away, it was the only way I knew how to help. Also, I felt she needed to deal with her feelings toward her father, who continued to torment her emotionally. Oh, he was wonderful to give Charlie and Mary great trips to exotic locations. It was a learning experience for them. But the price was emotional abuse. So much of what transpired on those trips I didn't learn about until years later. It seems there had been a lot of verbal abuse. I know how harmful that is. There are no visible scars, but the unseen scars on the heart last a lifetime.

At home, all was sort of under control. Robert, now fifteen, was doing well in school. He was never the squeaky wheel and was always a delight to the family (those are the ones to watch out for). Billy, my other stepson, now sixteen, was struggling in school. I found a high school which had a small school within the school for students who learn differently. I thought this might be helpful for him. Billy took a woodshop class and did really well in it. Rebecca was a prize stu-dent. Bill's two eldest children, Liane and Brian, were married and had started their own families. I was even a grandma to Alex, Liane's first child. It tickled me to go on the set to visit Bill with Alex bundled in my arms and have people think that Alex was Bill's and my daughter. I was forty-three at the time. Bill didn't like me to tell anyone how old

I was. He was upset when I had a fortieth birthday party and invited my oldest friends. I gave each of them a prize for being my friends for such a long time.

Bill and I took a weekend visit to Palm Springs. On a rainy day in the desert, we turned a nap into lovemaking. That day it rained not only outside, but on our parade. Something had happened to Bill physically that changed our marital relationship completely. There was nothing that could be done except a type of surgery that Bill didn't want to undergo. It was a very difficult time for us; we had had such a loving, sexual relationship. At the movies it became difficult to watch love scenes. I would look away—it was too painful and I noticed Bill looked away too. Walking through a lingerie department and touching the silk nighties was torture. I was upset that Bill didn't want to try the surgery, but I tried to understand. It was his body, but mine felt abandoned.

Through the years Bill knew I was always faithful to him, and he understood for the first time that he was loved for the person that he was, and for no other reason. Our relationship grew into something so special and so close. We always went to sleep wrapped in each other's arms and rubbing each other's foreheads until we fell asleep.

Mary came back from boarding school knowing that home was a better place to be. We had boundaries, which make children feel safe. I was so happy to have her back in the fold. Bill and I decided to try living at the beach, a more wholesome atmosphere for the children. Billy went back to live with his mother and finish school in town. John would now attend a Special Ed class in public school. I wanted desperately for him to be happy and healthy. We rented a beautiful blue Cape Cod home on a bluff overlooking the Pacific Ocean. The house was circled with daisies. On Sunday mornings, we looked out over the ocean and ate German apple pancakes. Mary and Robert were attending the same school and drove into town together. John rode bikes with his new friends and had roses in his cheeks again. All was well.

By the end of the summer, the Benedict Canyon house had been rebuilt and we had it on the market again. We also had our home in Brentwood on the market. But as luck would have it, the home in Brentwood sold and we were back in the canyon house again. We were still trying to find a home where the children would be in a neighborhood. Our next home was in Pacific Palisades, near the ocean. Always, it was important for Bill to have a tennis court. He was such a good player, and the children all enjoyed playing too. This house had a court and a guest room that was most often occupied by Bill's good friend, Jack Warden. What a terrific actor and wonderful story teller. We had the best family dinners! All the children talking at once, Jack trying to get a story in, and me correcting everyone's table manners. All the while Bill sat at the head of the table quietly drinking his two vodkas.

I was asked to do a play in Canada with Larry Linville, one of the stars from "M*A*S*H." It was a last-minute casting problem and I had to learn a two-character play in three days! They were trying it out in Palm Springs. Bill went with me to help me learn my lines. I told the children, "I can only talk to you if there is an emergency. That means blood!"

For three days and nights Bill and I ate, slept and breathed the lines from the play. I don't know how I made it through that first performance. I said the lines but I'm not sure they made much sense.

We decided I'd take John to Canada with me and spend my days tutoring him. It was really going to be the blind leading the blind. When we arrived in Canada we went to a bookstore. I asked John to choose any book he liked for us to read together. He chose a gruesome book on anatomy with popup pictures of the human body. I paid for the book and we walked out into the air, 40 degrees below zero. Our loveable dog, Harry, sort of Portuguese water dog, was with us. Most of all, he was sort of wonderful. He slept on my bed at night and kept my feet warm. We bought a coat for Harry to wear over his black fur. Boy, it was cold!

During the day we often went to the movies. I tried to find the most educational ones. At night, John sat in my dressing room while I was on stage and wrote a report about the movie we'd seen. In the morning we'd go over the report and circle the misspelled words. The word "dollar" was misspelled. I said, "John, that's an easy one. Just remember the little word doll, d-o-l-l, and add the little word or, o-r. Doll-or." I had him write it ten times. That evening, on our way to the theater, we passed a booth with a big sign, "Dollar Rent-A-Car." John poked me and said, "Look, Mom, they spelled it wrong. They spelled it d-o-l-l-a-r instead of o-r." I decided not to teach John spelling any more.

Bill came for Thanksgiving. The hotel staff, who didn't celebrate Thanksgiving, offered to bake us a Thanksgiving dinner. The turkey arrived and our mouths were watering.

"Ick, what's wrong with this turkey?" John hurried to spit it out.

"Honey, that's not nice. Why did you do that?"

"Taste it, Mommy."

Bill made a face and said," Yes, Honey. Taste it."

I did. "Yuck! It tastes like soap!"

We tried to be polite, but we just couldn't eat it. I nicely asked our waiter, "Excuse me, but the turkey tastes a little like soap."

"Yes, ma'am, it was washed in Dial first."

When the play closed, John and I were happy to be back home. But we had to face the problem of where he would go to school now. We decided seventh grade would be at the local public school. More tests were necessary for John to qualify for the special education class. He would have been totally lost in a regular classroom of his peers because his grade level for reading and math was more than two years behind. Poor guy, now he was in another new school. One day John came home from school and the housekeeper wasn't there. She thought I would be home, and I thought she would be there. When I did get home, about ten minutes after John had arrived, he was crying hysterically.

"John, honey, what's the matter? What's the matter?" He couldn't tell me, just kept crying.

"I thought everyone left me and they weren't coming back because I'm so stupid."

One night the children and I went to the movies in L.A. After the movie we went to C.C. Browns, an old ice cream parlor. As soon as we entered, someone in a booth said, "Hi there." It was Roger with his wife, JoAnne, and some friends.

"Oh, my. Hello. We just came in for some ice cream. How are you?" I certainly hoped I was being casual enough. There was polite chit-chat for a moment as I motioned to the children to find a booth.

There was that momentary feeling through me, but it passed. Roger was an old love, forever in my heart. But I was married and he was married.

*

My new purpose became to promote awareness about learning differences. I wanted to inform parents, teachers and students that children and adults who learn differently are not stupid or stubborn or bad, they just have a different learning style. I didn't want any child to suffer the way John had.

Bill became the most incredible support and help anyone could wish for. He gave me confidence in so many ways. He told me I was a good writer. I'd never really felt I was a good writer, but I liked to write. Bill would ask for suggestions when he was working on a show for TV.

"Do you think this is funny? What do you think would make it funnier?"

He was asking me? Me, who couldn't even spell? I would shyly make a suggestion and he would use it in the show. Eventually I became confident about my suggestions. Bill also helped me to think maybe I was pretty. Bill had a way of making people feel good. He really liked actors and would do anything as a director to make them feel comfortable in the role they were playing. It was just great to work with him professionally.

Bill's belief in me gave me the confidence to write a musical based on the lives of famous dyslexics, "Gifts of Greatness." In the

show were students at Landmark School for dyslexics, which John attended. Many Hollywood stars—Ed Asner, Pattie Duke, Julie Harris, Jack Warden, the Lennon Sisters, and Stephen Cannel—were in the

With Bill

cast. I directed the stage version and Bill directed a professional video. Not one star asked to be paid. The two men who wrote the musical score did it for love, and there was only one song that they didn't write, "Follow your Star," written by Roger Perry. I raised the money for the production and the video has been shown all over the world, even before the royal family of Spain. And I met the Queen!

Meanwhile, Robert and Mary graduated from high school. Robert, an artist, was accepted at Otis Parsons, a fine art school, and was now living with his mom. Mary went from Arizona to Kansas to college. Then she did something wonderful. To this day I remain proud and thankful that she had the wisdom to go to the Betty Ford Center in Rancho Mirage for family week. She planned it all and paid for it with her own money. At Betty Ford, a person may attend "family week" even if you don't have a family member going through treatment. You stay off campus and attend classes. There are small group classes to learn about alcoholism and the effects it has on family members. Then you have sessions with your family member, if you have one who is in treatment. If you don't have a family member there, you communicate to the absent person and express how his abuse of alcohol is affecting you and what you need from that person. It's an eye-opening experience.

Every night that Mary was there, she called to tell me how it was going.

"I think maybe I'm helping some of the parents here who have children in treatment. I sure hope so. I'm learning so much."

"I'm so proud of you, honey." Her last night there, she called to say good night.

"Oh Mommy, I really have learned a lot. I'm so glad I came."

"So am I."

"And you know what I learned?" She broke into tears. "I learned... I really am a good person."

"Oh, honey, I know you are. Please don't cry when I can't hold you. I love you so much."

She had been put down so often by her father, she didn't know she was a good person until strangers convinced her. Oh my sweet girl.

The Variety Club, owned by Milt Larson, was having a benefit that Bill and I attended. Guess who was on the program? JoAnne Worley with Roger Perry at the piano. Of course I had told Bill about my love affair with Roger, just as he had told me about his previous affairs. We enjoyed the show until JoAnne and Roger's number. While he was playing the piano, she was making derogatory remarks about him. Bill must have noticed how upset I was. I tried not to show my feelings, but Bill was always good about sensing when something was wrong. He asked if I wanted to leave. I nodded my head, yes.

When John turned eighteen, Ed no longer had the right to stop Bill from adopting John. It was a very proud day when Bill officially became John's dad. He certainly had been John's dad unofficially since John was five years old. Now it was John's turn to leave the nest. He had been working as an actor and doing very well. The world of make-believe, acting, writing, and directing was where he was headed. He had learned much from Bill. We helped him set up his studio apartment. It was an emotional day for me. We all had dinner together at home. Afterwards, we watched him walk to his car. I thought of the line Julie Harris said to him in "Gifts of Greatness": First I watched you learn to walk. Now I must watch you walk away.

We moved to a house in Malibu on the water. It was a butt-awful looking house painted mustard color, with poop brown trim. I knew it meant a lot to Bill to live at the beach and on the water. He hadn't been thrilled with the tennis court at the Palisades house. It didn't face exactly the correct way, north and south. It was a little off and it made Bill a little off too. Everyone in the family thought I had lost it, wanting to move to such an ugly house, even if it was on the water. I really surprised everyone with that makeover. I painted it gray with white trim, took down a wall that separated the living room from the dining room, and made a staircase between to create an open feeling. There was a stone fireplace in the living room and in the dining room, book-cases for all of Bill's leather-bound books. The children were promised those books when he died. His Emmys were placed on the shelf too. Our daughter-in-law, Jeanine, married to son Brian, is quite an artist. She did a lovely etched glass door for us that led to an outer courtyard. The master bedroom overlooked the ocean.

One day while I was on the telephone, I heard Bill casually call me.

"Just a minute, I'm on the phone."

"Honey, can you come here."

"Just a minute." I hung up and went into our bedroom, where Bill was lying across the bed. His upper body was on the bed but his feet were on the floor.

"What is it?"

"I can't move the left side of my body."

"I'll be right back, I'm calling the doctor." I tried to remain calm. I wasn't.

"Honey, can you make it to the car? The doctor wants to see you right away."

"Yeah, sure, if you help me. Just let me lean on you." With one hand on the railing and his left side propped up on me, we made it down the stairs. Robert was sitting on the sofa downstairs.

"Everything okay?"

Bill said, "Yeah, sure." I looked to Robert with grave concern as we walked by. I didn't want to alarm Bill by saying something to Robert.

In the car, I drove as fast as I could. The doctor looked at Bill and said, "Get him to St. John's hospital right away."

He helped me get Bill back into the car. I took off like a bat out of hell, traveling down Pacific Coast highway, one hand on the wheel and the other holding Bill's hand.

Dear God, please don't take him away from me. His usually tanned face had turned pale and gray. I drove up to the emergency room and got out of the car. The doors opened automatically and I screamed, "Heart Attack!!"

He had had a stroke. I spent the next few nights in the hospital, in a cot next to his bed. Never one to lose his sense of humor, when the nurse came in to take his blood pressure, he'd put my arm out instead of his. The only lasting result of the stroke was a slight limp in his left leg. Oh, he told great stories about that limp. Once he told someone he was hit by a surfboard; another time, it was a hockey stick. He didn't want anyone to know he'd had a stroke.

A few months later, he had another episode. John and I heard a crash and went running upstairs. Bill's body was rigid, his eyes rolled back in his head. When he came to, he started crawling on all fours. John and I got him down the stairs and into the car. I got behind the wheel and John sat with Bill in the back. As I pulled out of our driveway, the security guard came by, saw the situation and said he would drive us to the hospital. The drive along the Pacific Coast Highway seemed unending. Again, I ran into the emergency room yelling for help.

For several days, I stayed with Bill. He had had another small stroke. The nurse came in to talk about physical rehab. She wanted him to get started at the hospital and continue after he went home. He didn't seem to have any complications from the latest stroke, and he refused to go for physical therapy after we got home. I was afraid he would have another episode and fall down the stairs. We still wanted to live at the beach because it was so beautiful looking at the ocean. I found a large, more suitable house that still had the ocean view.

Bill started to abuse his medications and act drunk. I checked his medication and found that he had been taking double the recommended dose. He was still drinking his two vodkas and taking sleeping pills and antidepressants. I also discovered that he was seeing multiple doctors and getting drugs from each of them.

One day he wanted to go for a drive.

"Honey, that's not a good idea. You're pretty groggy from your medication."

"I don't know what you're talking about."

"I just don't want you to get into an accident and hurt yourself or someone else. Would you just let me talk to your doctor and see what he says?"

"Sure, go ahead. Here, help yourself to the phone. You want me to dial the number for you?"

I got the doctor on the phone and told him Bill had been doubling up on his medications and I was concerned about his driving.

"Just let him do what he wants."

Oh boy, did I ever feel angry and confused! Bill drove off.

This was the beginning of very belligerent behavior directed at John and me, Bill's nearest targets. The other children were off at school, and Robert and Billy lived in town with their mother. Things got worse. I was constantly worried about Bill. I insisted on driving my car if we were going somewhere. Bill started spending money as if we had an unending supply. I felt we needed to pull back on expenses, sell the large home at the beach and move into town, closer to hospitals. Those "white knuckle" drives to St. John's Hospital along the Pacific Coast Highway were too scary. Every time I drove home and saw an ambulance, my heart would pound, thinking Bill might be inside. The stress of Bill's illness, the conflict that had developed between him and John, and his distant attitude toward me seemed to be a catalyst for my migraine headaches, stomach aches, and mononucleosis. I even got typhoid fever!

*

A young man in Kansas City asked Mary to marry him. It was the man she had met the summer we all did "The Unsinkable Molly Brown." I reminded her that she had always wanted to have a winter in Colorado near her brother Charlie. "You don't want to wake up one day a married woman and wonder why you didn't have your winter in Aspen, Colorado." So she decided to spend a winter near her brother, working and skiing.

Bill and I took Robert on a trip to Boca Grande, Florida, a little island south of Sarasota. The National Dyslexia Research Foundation, for which I had become the Executive Vice President, had an office there. I just had a hunch Robert might love it there. He did, and shortly afterwards, Dana, his love, moved to be with him on the beautiful Gulf of Mexico. They married, built a home and started a family on the island.

Billy was repairing guitars and started his own business. I felt so proud of him and I also felt perhaps I had helped in his choice of a career. I had found the school where he learned woodcraft and had bought him his first guitar.

Bill and I moved to Mountain Gate, a lovely community on a hill near Westwood Village and UCLA. We were free from the Pacific Coast Highway, and near friends, doctor appointments and the hospital. Our place was a two-story townhouse connected to other houses, and we had a tennis court right outside our door. The house was much less expensive to maintain and a safer location for Bill, but he wasn't happy there. He called it a row house.

Bill was withdrawing more and more. The fear of losing him was always on my mind. I loved him so much! I needed to dive deep into something to occupy my mind. The Dyslexia Foundation kept me busy. We had a big fundraiser with Ringling Brothers Circus. The head of publicity for the circus asked if I would ride an elephant from the railroad station through downtown L.A. to the sports arena where the show would be. What fun, I thought! However, after two hours on the back of an elephant I climbed down and could hardly walk. Talk about bow-legged!

*

Whenever I was in New York City, I never failed to visit my fairy godmother, as I thought of Lillian Gish. Her health was failing, but her wonderful friend and manager, Jim Frasier, kept her life as full and joyful as it could be. The thought that Lillian and Helen, two wonderful ladies who had been so influential in my life, were getting ready to leave this life for another, made me feel lost. They were the best role models a young woman could have had. Their motto was "Live life to the fullest and give it all you've got!"

On my next trip to New York City, I visited Helen, now ninety-two. She was regaining her strength and feeling much better. We had so much to talk about. The happiest news was that Mary had fallen in love in Aspen with Kevin McClure, a good lad of Scottish descent, and Mary and I were having the best time planning her wedding. I told Helen about the engagement party Bill and I had hosted for her in Los Angeles.

"We had the party in the garden, and just before dinner I asked that we all hold hands for grace, and up on our hill we heard the sound of a bagpiper playing "Amazing Grace." He was dressed in full regalia. It was so beautiful! The neighborhood dogs started howling and the guests started howling too—with laughter."

"Oh, I can just imagine!"

"And the hit of the evening was Richard Sherman, our friend who composed 'Mary Poppins.' Well, he sat down at the piano and played songs from 'Winnie The Pooh,' which I had played for Mary when she was a little girl."

Helen was all smiles.

"After Mary was born, I'd stand here in the living room looking out at your beautiful rose garden and dream that one day she would have her engagement party here! How would you feel about that? I would arrange everything—you wouldn't have to do a thing. And if you aren't feeling well that day, you can watch the party from the window in your bedroom. With an engagement party here, your friends in New York and Nyack, who wouldn't be able to come to the wedding in Colorado, could share in the celebration."

Helen was overjoyed at the idea. The color rose in her cheeks and she started chatting like a magpie. "I'll fly everyone in for it. It will be a wonderful occasion! Oh, bless you, Joyce, to think of that. Oh dear, what shall I wear?"

We finished all the latest family news and I set my teacup down.

"I'll see you to the door," Helen said.

"Oh, no you don't, you stay right here. I certainly know my way out after all these years."

"No, no, I want to walk with you." I knew never to argue with Helen. She stood and almost lost her balance. I caught her by the arm and told her a silly joke. She was laughing as we walked through the living room. She stopped by the telephone table and picked up a whimsical angel figure.

"I want to give this to you, I don't know why." Then she thought a moment. "I can't, though. Someone gave it to me." I was that someone who had given it to her. But I didn't want to embarrass her. As we passed through the dining room, I glanced at the round table where I had spent so many wonderful and interesting dinners. I touched it solemnly, remembering each of the great ones in the history of the theater who had sat at this very table—Charlie MacArthur, Ben Hecht, Lillian Gish, Katherine Cornell, Bea Lillie, Ruth Gordon, and so many more. We walked through the butler's pantry and into the kitchen. At the windows, crisp blue and white curtains. I saw the big stove where Helen had made some good old homespun dinners, and there was the kitchen table we used to sit around and talk until the wee small hours.

Helen, a bit weary, held onto one of the kitchen chairs.

"I'm so excited about the party idea. We will talk and make plans. Isn't it wonderful—our Mary is getting married!" I gave her a kiss goodbye. It felt as if years had slipped back to another time when Helen had been "Mom" to me.

"Goodbye my dear, God bless." She stood waving at the screen door with a big warm smile on her face.

EIGHTEEN

Endings and Beginnings

On a snowy February day in 1993, I went back to Nyack to see Helen. Her health was failing and the family was concerned. What could I bring her for a gift, I wondered? On my first trip to Europe with Helen, we used to stand and drool as we looked into the windows of candy stores. Oh, that would be the perfect gift! I found some solid sugar Easter eggs, the ones you can look into and see a little scene. She used to collect eggs of all sizes. And of course, chocolate candies.

When I arrived, I went in through the familiar kitchen door. As the screen door slammed behind me, I dusted off the snow. Eileen, Helen's dear companion, came to greet me. I embraced her and gave her a box of chocolates. "You know your way," she said. I smiled and climbed the back stairs up to the second floor. Many memories flooded over me. The saddest one was holding Charlie in my arms and going downstairs to get a shot from the family doctor.

I tapped gently on Helen's open door. A nurse motioned me to come in. Helen was sitting by the window, her white hair the color of the snow falling outside. She seemed so much smaller to me. I reached over to give her a kiss and sat in a chair beside her. She had always been like a child about presents and gleefully unwrapped the chocolates and her Easter egg.

"Oh, you know, don't you? You smart girl. Remember how we used to walk by a chocolate store in Germany, then go back and stare in the window and groan? We had such fun together, didn't we?"

"Oh yes, we certainly did. I'll never forget it, and I'll always be so grateful to you."

Eileen brought us some tea and we talked about the children. It made me sad to see how small and weak she had become. I didn't want to tire her, so I didn't stay very long. I held her hand as I said goodbye.

"Oh, you don't have to go, do you? Can't you stay?"

I wanted to stay but I knew it was best not to visit too long. I kissed her goodbye. At the door I turned to look at her. She smiled. That was the last time I saw her.

Just a few days later, on February 27, Jim Frasier called to tell me my precious fairy godmother Lillian had passed away. She had been very ill, and over the last few years, I was afraid each time I saw her would be the last. I imagined God told Lillian she had to be in heaven first, to help Helen get in! Her funeral service was held in March at St. Bartholomew's, where Charlie had been christened. Jimmy, Lillian's godson, spoke lovingly at the service. Jim Frasier told me Lillian was cremated in the beautiful nightie I had given her. She was just short of her 100th birthday, an angel on earth and now an angel in heaven.

✳

After Lillian's funeral, I remained in New York. Charlie and Mary were in Nyack with Helen, who lay close to death.

It was St. Patrick's Day. As I waited to cross Fifth Avenue, the rain poured down around my umbrella. Just at that moment the Nyack School Band marched along, playing bagpipes. My thoughts went to Helen. I said a prayer for her and looked at my watch. It was 3:00.

When I reached the hotel, the red message light was blinking. It was Mary.

"Mommy, Grammy passed away at 3:00."

Nothing stays the same. Life is constantly changing. If you didn't hurt sometimes, if you weren't sad, you wouldn't be alive. I most definitely believe that God's plan is for the spirit to live on.

The day of Helen's funeral, I asked Jim if he planned to have bagpipes.

"I don't think so."

"Oh, she loved bagpipes."

"I know, but there's so much to take care of."

When Bill and I arrived in Nyack for the funeral, the limos were lined up outside the house. Jimmy asked me to go with him into the kitchen.

"I want to show you something. Years ago, Pop gave this valentine to Mom, and I'm going to put it in the casket with her."

As difficult as Jim had made my life and that of my children, at that moment I had only a feeling of love and concern for him.

"I have a surprise for you."

"What?"

"You'll see." He gave me a gentle smile.

The service was beautiful and I was proud of Mary and Charlie, who read from the Bible. We filed out of the church into a crisp day. The sky was so blue and the sun was shining. Just as Helen's casket was lifted into the hearse, I heard Jimmy's surprise in the distance: bagpipes. I knew Helen would be happy.

As the funeral procession traveled through the little town of Nyack, we could see how much she was loved. All the store fronts were draped in black bunting. As the hearse passed each store, the proprietors and shoppers came outside, took off their hats and bowed their heads.

At the gravesite Mary placed a sunflower on the casket, next to a small cross of white roses that I had sent. The sun shining on the glistening snow made it look like a field of diamonds. Helen lay next to her beloved husband, Charles MacArthur, and her daughter, Mary MacArthur. After saying my final farewell, I turned to look out at the Hudson River in the distance.

A young priest who had been very close to Helen during the last few years came up to me and took me by my shoulders. "Helen told me she had made your life very difficult at times, but she wanted you to know she loved you very much."

All the emotion, all the hurt and all the love welled up in me. Tears came, then uncontrollable sobs. Bill held me as I cried.

✳

A few weeks later, Jimmy called. He and H.B., his wife, wanted to go ahead with the party for Mary and Kevin in the rose garden. It was something Helen had looked forward to, and now they wanted to continue with the plans.

The day of the party was blistering hot. The leaves of the old trees high above the rose garden gave the only shade. H.B. had planned a lovely party. When dessert was served, it was strawberry shortcake— my very favorite, and the dessert Helen had prepared for me on my first visit to Nyack when I was just 16 years old.

I found H.B. "What a wonderful idea, to serve strawberry shortcake."

"Oh, it wasn't my idea, it was the caterer's."

I looked up to heaven and smiled. Oh, no it wasn't!

At home, Bill was becoming more and more difficult, angry about every little thing. His drinking, plus all the pills he was taking, caused him to act like a different person. I felt I needed some time alone because I was getting tired and depressed. I said, "Honey, I think I would like to visit with Charlie and Mary for a few weeks. It might be good for us to have a little break from each other. What do you think?"

"Sure, if that's what you want."

"It's not really what I want. I love you and I'll miss you. But I just feel I'm not making you happy. A little time apart might be good for each of us. I hope while I'm gone you might think about getting some help to make you feel better. I know one of your doctors is giving you antidepressant pills but, with the drinking and sleeping pills… " I didn't know where to go with the conversation. I hoped that while we were apart, he might realize he needed help.

"I think it would be good for both of us if you get help. You're not happy and I'm not happy. I love you."

Back in Colorado, seeing my children, taking long walks along the trails, breathing in the wonderful mountain air, I realized how tightly wound I'd been. I was relaxed and could laugh again. I spoke with Bill on the phone in the evenings. Each time I hung up, that tight feeling in my stomach came back. It was difficult trying to sleep after our talks.

Bill told me he was going to the Del Mar racetrack with some ladies from his beach movies. Maybe he was happier. But the racetrack and actresses from his movies didn't sound like the kind of help I hoped he would get.

Three weeks later, the phone rang.

Bill sounded desperate. "Honey, I need you to come right away. Please, you have to come right away!"

"Honey, I can't. Where are you? What's wrong?"

"You have to come right now! I need you!" He was sobbing. I started to panic.

"Where are you?"

"I'm in the Coronado Hotel in San Diego. You have to come!"

I tried to calm him down. I had never heard him like this. I thought he must be really drunk.

"I'm in Colorado. I'll try to get a flight out tomorrow. Now just lie down and go to sleep. You'll be fine. I have to go now. I'll talk to you in the morning, OK? Go to sleep now. I love you."

"I love you too."

I hung up but couldn't get back to sleep. I assured myself he'd be fine in the morning and finally fell asleep.

The next morning a very official-sounding person called and asked for Mrs. Asher. "I'm the doctor in ICU. Your husband is here. He almost died last night; it seems he was on a medication that shouldn't mix with red wine or cheese, and last night he had both. He had a massive seizure in his hotel room. His bed shook so hard it blocked the door. He's lucky he's alive."

"Will he be all right? May I talk to him?"

"Yes, I'll put him on."

"Hi honey, I guess I scared everyone here."

"You scared me too. Why would you have red wine and cheese? You knew you shouldn't!" I was angry because I was frightened.

"Oh, I'm fine. I can go home the day after tomorrow. Can you come get me?"

From everything I had learned, I knew it was now or never. When someone hits bottom, that's the time they realize they need help.

"Bill, you know you need help. I'll call some places where you can get treatment. You have to get help! I can't keep going on like this, and you could die. I'll get a flight out today and find the best place for you to go for help, okay?"

"Sure."

I called Betty Ford, St. John's and UCLA, all with excellent programs for addiction. Luckily, they had room. I called Bill. "Listen, they have room for you at Betty Ford, St. John's and UCLA. Which one would you like me to book?"

"Aaah, I don't want to go. If you just stay by my side I'll be fine."

"Bill, I love you. If you get help, I'll stay by your side the rest of your life. But if you don't, I have to leave. I can't keep doing this."

"I'll be fine, don't worry."

"You won't go?"

"No, you'll see—everything will be fine."

"I'll have John drive to San Diego and pick you up tomorrow."

This was going to be the hardest thing I ever had to do. I called all the children together and told them this was our only chance to try to work things out. "If I stay, your Dad is just going to keep going down this road to self-destruction, with me enabling him. If I leave, hopefully he will miss me, love me, and more important, love himself enough to get the help he needs. Tomorrow, John will pick him up at the hospital and I'll pack my car and drive to Colorado. I'll be gone when he comes home. I'm afraid if I see him, I won't be able to leave."

The next day I pulled out of the driveway and headed straight down the road. There was a feeling of great loss, as if someone was dying. But who? My heart was heavy as I drove along the highway to Las Vegas. The sky was very dark and foreboding, matching my sadness. Judy Collin's CD was playing. As I rounded a corner in the road, a small streak of sunlight shone through the dark clouds, as if God had cast a little light in the darkness. At the same moment Judy started to sing "Amazing Grace." I pulled to the side of the road and wept.

When I arrived in Vegas, I pulled into the Flamingo Hotel without a reservation. Alone in Vegas, a first! I decided to chase the blues away. I checked in and went to see if I could get a ticket to Cirque de Soleil. There was only one ticket left in the whole theatre, front center. I bought it! Just before the show I bought an ice cream cone. Ushered by one of the performers, I marched down the aisle to my seat, enjoying my ice cream and feeling very proud of myself. I had made this first step.

I arrived in Colorado on our seventeenth wedding anniversary. I had rented a condo in Snowmass. Lugging my suitcases up the stairs in the dark was quite a chore. Sadness took hold again. After unpacking, I looked around at the tattered furnishings. What could I do to make myself feel better and not give in to this sinking feeling? I had noticed a patch of daisies growing by the steps. I picked a single daisy, took it upstairs and placed it in a glass of water. I always said to my girls, "When you're feeling low, take a warm bath, put on a flannel nightie and have a nice cup of tea." So that's what I did! I found a kettle that was so rusted, the bottom fell out when I filled it with water. I boiled water in a pot and brewed my tea in a chipped china cup from the cupboard. I placed the flower and teacup on the table and pulled out the rickety chair to sit on. I sat down, looked at the daisy, took a sip of tea, and leaned back in the chair. "You're gonna be all right." Just then, the back of the chair gave way and I fell "ass over tea cups!"

✳

Originally, Mary's wedding was to be in Los Angeles. However, when I knew I had to stay away from Bill, I asked Mary and Kevin if they would marry in Colorado. They agreed. Mary wanted both Jim and Bill to walk her down the aisle. Mary loved Bill and felt he had given her all the love and respect that Jim never did. I had to shame Jim into paying for half the wedding. He was going to let Bill pay for the whole thing!

Jim would have no part of sharing the fatherly role. He wanted to walk down the aisle alone with Mary. Mary asked if I could walk with him. Again, Jim refused. It was upsetting to Mary, but we didn't want to make waves. It had been hard enough to get Jim to pay for at least part of the wedding. The night before the wedding, Mary, my mother, and I all climbed into a great big old featherbed in the historical Jerome Hotel in Aspen. A gentle snow fell outside. Inside, three generations snuggled together, giggling like schoolgirls.

The next day, the room filled with activity. Mothers, grandmothers, bridesmaids, godmothers, all getting ready for the big day. I couldn't help crying when I helped Mary put on her veil. When she was all dressed and looking beautiful, I stood by while Jim came in the room and had a moment with her. He had tears in his eyes and said, "You look so pretty."

After he left, Bill came in. He stood for a moment at the door looking at her, speechless. Then he walked over, took her hands and kissed them. One sweet loving gesture said it all.

Mary looked radiant as she walked down the aisle. At the end of the ceremony, she stopped and gave Bill a kiss. We danced the evening away with family and friends. I looked out at all my children, all eight. I was so very happy.

Bill and I sat side by side, holding hands during Mary's wedding. I thought if he won't get the help he needs, maybe we can at least stay married, live separately and see each other from time to time. I missed him so much when we weren't together.

On reflection, I think instead of fixing our marriage and our different styles, we fixed new houses. Instead of focusing on our problems as man and wife, we focused on our children's problems, or at least I did. And yet we loved each other very much. Earlier times often found us laughing so hard we would have to pull over to the side of the road. We'd sit a moment, get control of our laughter, pull onto the freeway, look at each other and start laughing all over again. It was this laughter that saw us through many difficult times, but the laughter became less frequent and the silence more and more.

As I walked in the mountains of Colorado, I remembered all these moments. Our phone calls always ended with "I love you." One night after a phone call, I lay my head down, exhausted from the effort of making myself stay away from him. His speech would sometimes sound slurred, and at those times I hung up and cried. I thought being away was the only way to help both of us.

Eventually, I felt emotionally strong enough to go back to Los Angeles and work out a settlement agreement with Bill. I told him I had no intention of getting divorced. We sat next to each other in the attorney's office. Bill felt he should take care of me because of the years I had looked out for his children and because he knew how much I loved him. There were times sitting with Bill and the attorney that I thought Bill was giving me too much. Still, I hoped we could find a way to be together.

In Snowmass I bought a condo and set to work fixing it. When I finished, it looked pretty good, and cozy. In the early mornings, I would sit in bed with a cup of tea. In longhand I started to write my story. Some days were good, living in Colorado near my children. But after visits with Bill, depression walked beside me and my steps became heavy and slow. Mary said, "Mom, I wish you would go to Betty Ford and try to work out all the feelings you're having." Such a wise girl. A few days later, I was on the overnight train, headed for Betty Ford family week in Rancho Mirage, near Bill in Palm Desert.

I sat up in coach all night, nodding off only occasionally. The sound of the train's click! clack! click! as it chugged along through the Colorado mountains soothed me. I was on a journey to learn how to be stronger and to understand myself. It was a frightening prospect— very frightening!

Whenever I thought about my life as a child, going from foster home to foster home, I would feel sorry for myself, so I chose not to think about it. The same with my unhappy marriages—I chose not to dwell on them. Now I would be forced to look at myself and learn to deal with my feelings in a different way. I didn't want to open my heart to the pain; I was afraid once I did, I would start crying and never be able to stop. The way I had always coped was to put on a smile. I found that if you smiled you felt better inside. We all wear masks, and mine was a smile.

At Betty Ford in a group session, I relayed a sad instance from one of my marriages. The whole time I told the story, I had a smile on my face. The facilitator of the group said, "Why are you smiling? What you are telling us is very sad."

I grinned self-consciously. "Yes, I know."

"Tomorrow, I want you to feel what you are saying and not smile all day."

That was the hardest assignment because I felt naked without my smile. Needless to say, I wasn't able to do it all day, but it made me get in touch with my feelings, and I did cry. In my marriages, I was so caught up in making things look good, I didn't feel the pain myself. Now I learned that the co-alcoholic, me, gets sick right along with the alcoholic. That explained a lot about the migraine headaches, mono-nucleosis, and stomach aches that I had had. The real trial was not to go see Bill. He knew I was at Betty Ford. I wanted him to know, in the hopes he would go too. At night he called the Holiday Inn where I stayed. I held strong by not going to see him. Little by little, I felt stronger and more able to cope.

After some time back in Colorado, I felt ready to visit Bill. I drove to Palm Springs and had dinner with him. Later, while he smoked a cigar and sipped brandy, we sat out on the golf course looking at the stars and talking. When it was time for bed, I went to the guest room and he tucked me into bed, just like I was his little girl. On the next visit, we went to Ruth's Chris Steakhouse for dinner. There was a very pretty hostess there, and Bill and I stopped to say goodnight to her on our way out.

Bill said, "This is my wife. She lives in Snowmass, Colorado, and I live here. You want to go out?" Bill was always flirting and had quite a few lady friends. His housekeeper kept me posted on his dating life, especially when she was concerned about who he was seeing. She told me once he was dating a mud wrestler. Oh, well, that's my Bill! He was on his path and I was on mine. Bill asked the hostess at Ruth's Chris out to dinner. They went out often.

One night, after we had been separated for a couple of years, Bill called.

"You remember the gal we met at Ruth's Chris one night?"

"Yes, of course. You asked her to go out."

"Well, I want her to move in. I really need someone. But she won't move in unless I get a divorce."

I was quiet.

"Are you OK with getting a divorce?"

"Yes, of course, if that's what you want."

"But I'm worried about you losing your health insurance."

This wasn't how I wanted it to be, but I knew Bill needed help and it would be better for him not to be alone. It didn't seem he would ever get the help I thought he needed, and this lady seemed very nice. "Sure, I'll be fine. Don't worry." I needed to hang up before I started to cry. Six months later, the day after our divorce was final and a month before our twentieth wedding anniversary, Bill and Meredith were married.

A few months later, Meredith asked if I would help plan Bill's 75th birthday. It was to be a surprise, and she didn't know all of his friends. So she and I and all the children put our heads together and planned a grand celebration at Liane and Eric's home. The children came early in the day to decorate, using a beach party theme because Bill had written and directed all the "Beach Party" movies. Bill's first wife, Dorothea, known as Danni, came, and I was there with a friend, Bill Wesson. The grandchildren thought because we were such a big and confusing family, it would be fun to make buttons for everyone to wear.

Danni's button and mine said "I was married to Bill Asher," Meredith's button said "I am married to Bill Asher," and all of the other ladies at the party had buttons that said "I'm not married to Bill Asher… yet!"

The children wore labels: "I'm daughter #1 from marriage #1," or "I'm daughter #2 from marriage #3," or "I'm son #3 from marriage #2," and so did the grandchildren. What a great idea, what fun! I assembled photos into a video of Bill's life, capped off with Bill and Meredith's wedding picture. When the birthday cake appeared, Danni and I sang "Happy Birthday" all slow and breathy, the way Marilyn Monroe sang to President Kennedy at Madison Square Garden on his birthday. (Bill had directed that gala for Kennedy.)

David Capell, one of our old friends, took in the combined family of children, grandchildren and wives, all laughing and having a wonderful time together, and said, "This is the true meaning of one big happy family."

One day, an old friend from Theatre East, Tom Bellin, called. He said he was working on a musical with Roger Perry and was interested in having me direct it. I was stunned. Roger? I could work with Roger?

"Well, that would be fun. You know I live in Colorado now."

"Yes, I got your number from Norman Cohen. Any chance you might be coming into town so we could meet?"

I would get to see Roger! I must brush aside all the cobwebs of past memories. I knew he was still married to JoAnne, and I certainly had no desire to interfere with his marriage. I knew he had a drinking problem—I wasn't ever going down that path again. But it would be so good to see him after all these years!

"Sure, when would you like to meet? Could you send me the script first?"

A few weeks later, sitting in Jerry's Deli below Theatre East, I waited for Tom and Roger. I spotted Roger and his wonderful smile from across the room. Those blue eyes. Oh dear, butterflies again.

"There you are!" He leaned over to give me a kiss on the cheek.

Tom came around the corner and joined us. After discussing the play, I asked if JoAnne approved of me as director. I knew she wasn't fond of me, probably because of my past relationship with Roger. Roger assured me JoAnne was fine with my directing. I hoped past grievances were really past. (By the way, JoAnne had said, "No way!" to my directing Roger's musical.) After Tom left, Roger asked if I'd like to have a glass of wine with him. I was happy to have the chance to tell him how much he had meant in my life.

"Remember that day, years ago, when you came to my trailer to tell me you were going to have a baby?"

He looked puzzled. "Yes. I still don't know why I did that."

"Well, I decided to have a baby too. That's my Mary. Then after you broke up with me, I married Ed Mallory and had John. So you see, indirectly, I have you to thank for two of my wonderful children."

"That's great, I'll drink to that."

After returning to Colorado, I got a few notes from Roger. Each time, I felt a flutter at the sight of his handwriting. He sent a CD of "It's Your Time to Curtsy and My Time to Bow," a song he had written for his daughter Dana's wedding. Another card said, "Just thinking of you."

It was uplifting to hear from someone I had loved for such a long time.

*

Mother had become very ill, and I moved her and her favorite nurse to stay with me in Colorado. We had frequent ambulance trips to the hospital, charging through the blinding snow in the middle of the night. One night the doctor said she needed to be in a nursing home. With a sinking feeling, I filled out forms for the nursing home, as if I were doing the same thing my mother had done to me when she put me in foster care.

On my next trip to Los Angeles, I saw the screening of a film that John directed. I was so proud of him! The screening went very well and I went to bed thankful he was able to do what he had always dreamed of.

Late that night, the phone shattered the silence. Mary, calling from Colorado, said shakily, "Mom, they think Fifi's dying."

A sharp pain hit the pit of my stomach. I stopped breathing.

"I'm leaving right now. What time is it there?"

"It's four-thirty. You could probably get a six o'clock plane."

My brain was going a mile a minute. With my free hand I pulled off my pajama top. Panic started to set in.

"Mary, honey, please go be with Fifi. I don't want her to be alone."

"Mom, I'm sorry, I don't think I can. I'm sorry, I'm sorry."

I could hear how frightened she sounded, like a little girl again.

"That's all right, honey, I understand. I'll call Bill Wesson."

I looked at the photograph on my bedside table, two radiantly happy faces, Mother and Dad. Now she was dying and I wasn't there to hold her hand and tell her how much I loved her.

The phone rang again. It was Bill.

"Your mother's gone. I got there just minutes after she died, but it was very peaceful. There was no pain. She just went to sleep."

Words that change your whole life; the person who gave you life is gone.

"Oh, please don't let them take her away, please," I begged him.

"I'll stay with her until you get here."

The taxi was waiting out front. It was still dark and pouring rain. I asked the driver to get to LAX as fast as possible and, for the first time, said the words "my mother just died." This dear little man drove through two stop lights and sped to the airport. Alone in the back of the cab I felt like the abandoned little girl I once was.

As I watched raindrops run down the window of the airplane, I couldn't make out which were raindrops and which were my tears. We taxied down the runway, leaving behind the dark rainy morning and rising through the clouds into one of the most beautiful sunrise skies I had ever seen. It was as if I was being lifted upward just as my mother's soul was being lifted from her body into God's loving arms.

When I landed in Aspen, Mary was waiting. She smiled with all the strength she could muster. We held each other tight.

"Bill is with her and they're waiting for you. Kevin and the baby are in the car."

I saw my grandson Ford in his car seat. Kevin came around to give me a hug and put my bag in the car. Suddenly I wanted to take Mother a long-stemmed ruby rose. I knew that she would wait for me to give her that last gift of love. "Kevin, hurry! I have to hold her and tell her I love her! But could we please stop at the flower shop? I want to get a rose."

After a quick stop for the rose, I sat in the car holding Ford's little hand just as he had held Mother's. In the last two years of her illness, he used to wrap his hand around her finger and look into her eyes. They seemed to share a secret, as if he knew where she was going.

So many emotions! Be brave. This is nature. She's with God.

I half expected Mother to greet me when I entered her room. Maybe there was a mistake, and she would say, "Joyce, what a pretty rose. Your Dad always brought me ruby roses."

Bill waited at the foot of the bed. I saw Mother lying very still, a white sheet folded neatly over her legs. She wore the flowered nightie I had bought her, and around her neck was the single pearl necklace I had given her on her eighty-third birthday. Mary had placed a bouquet

Mary, me, and mother; we miss her

of pink roses beside the pillow. The windows were open and a soft breeze blew the curtains.

Leaning down, I wrapped my arms around her. She didn't open her eyes and say "Joyce." Never in my life had I wanted so much to hear my name. The sobs that I had held inside started up in waves of agony, as if coming from another body. Finally I wiped my tears, stood up, and asked for a few minutes alone. Mary and Bill left. I placed the red rose in Mother's hand. I took a couple of the pink roses and, pulling one petal at a time, scattered them over my mother's body. As each petal fell, I told her I loved her and thanked her for all the things she had done for me.

I stood back and looked at her, covered in pink rose petals, with the red rose in her beautiful hands. Still, she didn't say "Joyce."

My mother was gone.

*

On a snowy day when I was picking up my mail at the post office, there was that handwriting again, a postcard from Roger. "I have gone to hell." What in the world? I called Norman to find out. Norman said Roger had gone to The Betty Ford Clinic.

"Oh that's great. That's wonderful news!"

"Yes, it is."

"Thanks, Norm, for letting me know."

"I think he would want you to know."

Another post card. "I'm learning a lot, sometime I'll tell you. Love, Roger."

About a month later, I received a bouquet. "I hope these are Columbines. If I remember, they're the Colorado state flower. Love, Roger."

In his next letter, Roger suggested I write to him at a different mail box number, as JoAnne sometimes picked up the mail. Roger had intimated that his marriage wasn't going very well since Betty Ford. JoAnne sometimes falsely accused him of drinking. I tried to assure him things would work out. He said she would be upset after she'd been on the road working, that she'd come home and start finding fault. I suggested he have the house ship-shape, with flowers waiting for her. Later he wrote that she complained about the tuxedo tie he wore. I found the tie he needed and sent it to the secret mailbox.

JoAnne and Roger had been married almost 24 years. Roger said they were in therapy together and he was trying hard to work things out.

The good times really started to roll in the family. In addition to Mary and Kevin's baby, Dana and Robert had a daughter, Ella. Charlie, named by "Skiing Magazine" as one of the top 100 ski instructors in America, was teaching such notables as Vice President Gore's family. Billy had a very successful guitar store in Los Angeles. Eric, Liane's husband, won an Emmy for editing, and their two girls, Alex and Megan, were growing up to be beauties. Brian and Jeanine had two great kids, Keala and Keith. Rebecca was a successful script supervisor and had worked alongside her brother John, now 28, who had just completed directing the film "Diamonds," with Kirk Douglas, Dan Aykroyd and Lauren Bacall. Was I proud? You bet!

On my birthday I was doing a bit part in John's film, playing a waitress in a Reno casino. My costume was short and revealing, a change from the characters I usually played. When I came on the set, I couldn't help but tease John. In front of his entire crew I said, pointing to my breasts, "Hey, John, remember these?" John turned scarlet. "Mom!"

After the shoot, John, Rebecca, and Kirk Douglas appeared with a huge birthday cake. While they sang "Happy Birthday," I read the words on the cake: "You're the star of our life. We love you. Rebecca and John." John hugged me and my eyes welled with tears. "What's the matter, Mama?" I held him and thought of all he'd been through to get to where he was now. I thought my heart would burst with joy.

I was busy going back and forth to Los Angeles. One of those occasions was John's wedding to Jenny McCarthy, a big celebration with all the family. Bill and Meredith sat next to me in the front row. Rebecca and Mary were bridesmaids, and as they came down the aisle, Bill waved, his glass of vodka safely stashed under his chair. During the ceremony he yelled out once in a while, "Way to go John! Good luck this time! Good lookin' gal you got there!"

At the end of the reception, a staff person at the Beverly Hills Hotel handed me a message and said, "We were told not to give this to you until the reception was over."

I opened the note, from my sister, Linda. "Call right away, no matter how late it is." This was not going to be good news. Daddy had passed away. This time Daddy was gone forever.

NINETEEN

At Last

'd never had a chance to do much dating. A child of the fifties, I went from one marriage to another. If I slept with someone, I thought I had to marry him. Silly me! Now I was determined to get to know men without getting entangled. You'd think after three marriages to difficult men, I would know better, but once again I got involved with a charming, handsome, adventurous guy, who unfortunately was also an unpredictable, moody control freak. I enjoyed all the attention—he was very good at courtship—and we had exciting times. But he was not good for me. Sex became the basis of our relationship. Sometimes he accused me of things he made up! I thought I was going crazy. Breaking up, getting back together—it was confusing and I felt ashamed of myself. Then after a month without contact, he would ask me to a romantic evening out, which always ended in bed.

Again, I went to see a therapist. I tried to explain the relationship to her and told her I was frightened. She said, "Men like him are

very cunning. Sexually they can be compelling, but they are dangerous. Whenever you see him, just picture *Danger* written across his
forehead."

After a stormy fight during which he threatened me, my therapist
arranged for me to go to a shelter for victims of abuse and then to a
treatment center. I felt embarrassed, defeated and just plain stupid.
At the shelter, my counselor gave me a big hug. I slumped onto the
bed, where I found a book, "The Gift of Fear." I explained what had
happened. My counselor suggested I get treatment for codependency.
I needed it, obviously! She and I choose Cottonwood in Arizona. I
called Charlie to tell him I was going away for treatment. I was filled
with shame, but he and Mary were very understanding.

I arrived at Cottonwood on a hot day in July, when the other
residents were all in group sessions. I signed in. Someone offered to
carry my suitcase, but I said I could manage. My soul felt as heavy as
my suitcase. I walked along the dusty path to the room I had been
assigned and felt this was part of the punishment I had inflicted upon
myself for having sex without love and for choosing so badly again.
When I opened the door and saw the beds lined up facing each other,
in a flash I remembered the day when I was seven years old and first
saw the beds lined up in the orphanage.

I lay on the bed and looked at the ceiling, my eyes filled with tears.
I don't recall anything about my roommates, maybe because I needed
to concentrate solely on my own problems. For four weeks, I studied
and learned the twelve-step program. How important it is to believe in
a higher power, as I already did. "God, grant me the serenity to accept
the things I cannot change, the courage to change the things I can, and
the wisdom to know the difference." The hardest thing I had to do was
to write a letter forgiving myself, and read it to my group. I am always
able to forgive others. Why is it so hard to forgive oneself?

*

Back home in Aspen, even after everything I'd learned at Betty Ford and Cottonwood, I allowed this man back in my life. It's unbelievable to me now, but two months after seeing him again, I agreed to marry him. He was down on his knee, holding a ring, and although my inner voice shouted "No!!" I agreed. The marriage was short and frightening. He became more and more controlling, dictating my daily schedule and demanding to know where I was at all times. I was walking on eggshells and losing all respect for myself. My children were alarmed for me too. During the brief time with him, we rented an apartment in Los Angeles. I was very frightened; I called Norman.

"Oh Norman, I've done something terrible! My family's upset with me and I'm really frightened. I don't know what to do." I told him I was in Los Angeles with my scary, unpredictable husband. Then he told me that Roger and JoAnne were getting divorced and that Roger had moved out.

"Is he OK? Should I give him a call?"

"I'm not supposed to give anyone his telephone number, but I think he'd like to hear from you. He's staying at the Holiday Inn in Glenwood."

What a shock. I knew things hadn't been going to well for Roger and JoAnne, but I didn't know the extent. I called the Holiday Inn and asked for Roger Perry. When he answered, for a moment I was at a loss for words. Hearing his voice was like walking into a warm, welcoming home and finding a comfortable chair by the fire. I wanted that warm feeling to wash over me for another moment.

"Hello," he repeated.

"Hi, Roger, it's Joyce."

Now it was his turn to take a moment before he spoke.

"Well, well. This is a nice surprise. How did you find me?"

"Norman, of course."

"Of course. Where are you?"

I told him I was in town and wanted to know if he was all right. We planned to meet for lunch the next day. After I hung up, I realized those funny, flopping butterflies weren't in my stomach, only a sense of calm.

Roger looked relaxed and terrific, his blue eyes bright and clear, set with purpose. I gave him a big hug. Those arms, once so familiar and strong, were hugging me once more. All I could think was … you are my home.

We followed the hostess to our table. When the waitress came to take our order, she said, "I have never seen two people so in love." We turned to each other and smiled. How did she know?

Roger told me he had been unfaithful to JoAnne, and that prompted his wanting to go to Betty Ford; he wanted to get sober and work on his marriage. Sadly, it hadn't worked for the marriage. He hadn't had a drink now for four years. No wonder he looked so well!

We talked for a long time and I told him how happy my marriage to Bill had been, and how sadly it had ended. "But Bill is married now and I'm glad he has someone to look after him. The best thing about our marriage was I had a brood of children to raise, and having such a big family made me very happy." Roger remembered working with Bill and what a nice guy he was.

I asked about Roger's children, Chris and Dana, and I talked about Charlie, Mary and John.

Roger, proud father, had sent me a picture of Dana in her wedding gown—a lovely bride. Chris was living in Yucca Valley, north of Palm Springs, and he played piano at church. It was good to hear about those two. I remembered them as little rascals when Roger and I dated so many years ago.

I told Roger about my recent, impulsive marriage. "I don't know how I ever got involved with him." Roger said, kindly, "You were very vulnerable. Your parents had just passed away. He just caught you at a difficult time in your life."

It was time to put everything I'd learned at Betty Ford and Cottonwood into practice. I had to learn to protect my boundaries and get myself untangled. I filed for divorce. I called a realtor in Aspen and asked her to put my condo on the market. The next call was to ask a friend to pack up my condo because I was moving to L.A. I told her, "As fast as I can, this cowgirl is getting out of Dodge!"

Our tree

*

Safely ensconced in my new apartment in Los Angeles, and with everything wrapped up in Aspen, Roger and I started dating. Very slowly at first, baby steps.

I asked him if he remembered the maple tree we had planted a long time ago.

"I drive by it all the time."

"You do! So do I!"

"It's huge, isn't it?"

"Yeah, about as tall as this building. It was only about five feet when we planted it."

We went to the movies, ate hamburgers, and saw plays. It was a little frightening to be with someone you had thought about so often, and cared about so much. Someone you had once been close to. Someone who had never left your heart. How could he live up to my romantic dreams? How could I live up to his romantic dreams?

Each time Roger took me home after an evening out, we would give each other a hug and a little goodnight kiss. Neither one of us could handle more at the time. Roger, always the gentleman, didn't press for more. It was comforting being two old friends together again. Besides, trying to repeat the passion of the past would be exhausting at our ages, sixty-three and sixty-seven.

Not that I didn't think about those magical nights of love so long ago. Eventually, it happened. After thirty-two years, we were lovers again! Believe me, he lived up to all my romantic dreams!

The Dyslexia Foundation was holding a fundraising conference in Greece. As Executive Vice President, I had been there to scout the location and had to go back as hostess. My responsibilities included arranging a group dinner. A cruise would follow the conference.

I asked Roger if he'd like to go with me, explaining that I would be very busy entertaining the guests. They would have to be my first concern. If he understood that, it would be wonderful to have him join us. He said he understood and would like to go. The first night in Greece, there was a cocktail party to welcome the attendees. I made sure that Roger was comfortable with a glass of soda and a view of the water. Then I greeted the attendees.

I checked on Roger to see if he needed another soda. But when I looked over at him and smiled, he returned my smile with an angry look.

Trying to cheer him up, I asked if he would like to go to dinner with some friends.

"How many people are going?" He sounded irritated.

"Just the headmaster of a school and his wife. I'd like you to meet them; they're old friends."

"All right."

Roger said not one word during dinner. I was upset because I wanted my friends to see what a wonderful man I was dating. But no, he was sullen and withdrawn. I tried to act unconcerned and plowed through the dinner as best I could.

The next morning, I asked Roger, "What happened last night? Why were you so cranky and cold?" He started blaming me for his behavior. "You should have told me you were going to be busy. And there were so many people."

"I did tell you! I warned you that on this trip I would have to be the hostess. You said you understood."

"Well, you should have told me it was going to be a cocktail party and everyone would be talking about dyslexia all the time!"

At Cottonwood I had learned not to let people "should upon me," not anymore! Very firmly I said, "Roger, I don't think this is going to work out. I think you'd better get a flight off the island right away."

"If you make me leave, I'll start drinking again!"

"That is your problem." I walked away. (The old Joyce would have said, "Oh no, I'm sure we can work things out. Please don't leave! I didn't mean it.") This was a big turning point for me. I really meant what I said!

I didn't go back to our room all day. There was no way I would go through this kind of nonsense, ever again! When evening came, I returned to the room and was upset to see Roger still there. He looked at me like a little boy who had done something wrong and wanted to explain.

"Don't be upset, I was on the phone all day trying to get a flight off the island. There isn't a flight leaving for two days. But I really want to say how wrong I was. I'm really sorry. You're right, you told me what to expect. I really am sorry, and I'm sorry I couldn't get a flight right away. I'm so sorry."

"Well, I guess there's nothing we can do." Over dinner, we discussed our feelings. What I didn't know at the time, but learned later, was that recovering alcoholics have a hard time at cocktail parties. Especially with lots of people they don't know, who are talking about things they aren't involved in. Roger, only four years into recovery, had allowed himself to be put into a situation that he knew could be a "slippery slope" into wanting a drink.

We decided to see how the next few days would go. Everything went so well—thank God there had been no flights off the island!

Shortly after we returned from the trip, Roger went to visit his daughter in Nashville. Roger told Dana that we were seeing each other, and we had fallen right back into being in love after all these years. It was a different kind of love, a deeper, more mature love—but nevertheless, love. I treated myself to a solo trip to Newport Beach. I rested, swam, sat in the sun and thought about Roger.

Summer was around the corner and we thought it would be fun to rent a house near Aspen. We would be able to go to the music festival and spend time with Charlie, who had married an Australian Lassie, and Mary and the grandchildren. We found a house in Carbondale with a front porch and rocking chairs. Each morning, we enjoyed coffee on the porch and a view of Mount Sopris.

Being with Roger was, in a word, wonderful! For two years we lived together in Los Angeles, visited our children, and traveled as entertainers on Seaborne cruises. For a while I gave enrichment lectures about "The Mary Tyler Moore Show." This is silly, I thought. Here I have Roger, who plays the piano and sings beautifully. So I asked the cruise director if she would like to have Roger and me entertain. She loved the idea! I ended up writing two shows. "My Life Upon the Wicked Stage," a multi-media show with photos, film clips and Roger at the piano, wove our love story with stories about acting. The other show was "Remembering Helen Hayes with Love," the intimate story of my relationship with the First Lady of American Theatre. We sailed all over the world. How lucky we were!

Each summer we drove to Colorado to spend a few months with all the children. On our way, we stopped in the desert to see Bill, by then in a wheelchair. During those visits we would take Meredith and Bill to dinner. Bill was still drinking quite a bit and his health was in decline. At the end of the evening I always gave him a big hug. I would sit silently for a moment, remembering how he had been so strong, so active, playing tennis every day. If only he'd been able to get the help he needed, he might have been able to continue the activities he loved. I voiced my concern to Roger, who knew how much I loved Bill. Because Roger is so secure in my love for him, he has always understood.

In the fall of 2002, Roger and I, hand in hand, walked through the golden Aspen trees. What a sight to behold! It looked as if God had thrown a handful of golden coins down from heaven.

I asked, "Do you think we'll ever get married?"

Without a beat he said, "Sure."

"Oh, really? When?"

"In the spring."

"This spring?"

"Yeah."

"I'd better start planning." And I did!

We decided to get married in the church we had been going to in Westwood. I was excited because my mother's sister, Aunt Billie, with whom I had such wonderful times as a child, was coming with cousin Linda and two of my three sisters, Susan and Linda and their children, all the way from Florida. Bill and Meredith and all my Asher children and grandchildren were going to be there. Roger's children and my children and grandchildren would all attend, along with our old friends, who had called us "star-crossed lovers."

What would I wear? I had worn white for my first wedding, pink my second wedding, sea foam green my third wedding (doesn't that sound awful?). I had never worn yellow, so that's what I chose!

Very early the day before the wedding, my two sisters, Ed's sister, Carol Ann, my friend Caryl and I went to the downtown flower mart. I picked out the flowers, and they helped me arrange two smaller bouquets on the altar and two giant ones on either side. I made all the bouquets for the wedding party to carry. What fun it was to be doing this with four of the dearest people in my life! The whole time I was thinking about how lucky I was to be marrying the man I had loved so much and for so long. He hadn't had a drink for six years.

The night before the wedding we had a rehearsal dinner, complete with mariachi music, at a Mexican restaurant, Roger's favorite. Everyone had a great time and applauded the cake—"Roger and Joyce At Last."

On April 27, 2002, the wedding party gathered at the church. Just before Norman walked me down the aisle, I whispered to him, "I don't know why, but I'm so nervous."

"I don't know why either; you've been waiting for this for 35 years!"

Chris Carothers sang, "If it takes forever, I will wait for you, for a thousand summers I will wait for you."

Norman put my hand in Roger's. The minister asked, "Who gives this woman to be married to this man?" Norman answered, "Her children and I do."

At the altar were Mary, my Matron of Honor, Roger's daughter, Dana, his son Chris, who was Best Man, and Charlie, John and Ford, the ring bearer. My granddaughters, Ruby and Daisy, were flower girls. Alex, my eldest granddaughter, read something beautiful and meaningful that she had written for us.

Roger's friend and mine, Ron James, told the story about the maple tree.

"Thirty-five years ago, Roger and Joyce planted a little maple tree, about five feet high. When they got together again, she asked Roger if he had seen how big that tree had grown. Today that maple tree is about three stories high and as wide as this church. Roger doesn't know it, but hanging from the end of every pew, and in every bouquet, are leaves from that maple tree that Roger and Joyce planted so many years ago."

My, so much has happened since our marriage. Sad things and happy things. But, without the rain, there would be no rainbows. We lost our dear friend Norman, followed by the loss of many other dear friends. That is the most difficult thing about getting old, losing your friends.

Our rainbows have been many. We are now a combined family of 10 children and 14 grandchildren and one great-grandchild. Remember that Roger was put up for adoption when he was two years old. With granddaughter Alex's help, he was able to unite with his sister, who had been looking for him for seventy-two years!

At last, after so many years, we're together! We feel it's a miracle. Our close-knit family helps each other in times of need and celebrates each other in times of joy. I'm so very grateful.

I have found my "home sweet home." You see, there can be a happy ending!

Appendix

A little bit of information that I hope may be helpful to you as it has been for me:

- **HAZELTON BETTY FORD CENTER AND FOUNDATION**
  Support programs for children and families
  Addiction—treatment-recovery—education
  Rancho Mirage, CA

- **COTTONWOOD – TUCSON:**
  Addiction Rehab and Behavioral Health Treatment Center in Arizona. An inpatient holistic behavioral health treatment center. A place to find understanding, healing and hope.

+ **THE DYSLEXIA FOUNDATION**

The Dyslexia Foundation is a nonprofit organization that assists children and adults with dyslexia to avoid the suffering caused by reading failure so they may reach their full potential.

Books

I've read so many self-help books—these are just a few:

+ **EACH DAY A NEW BEGINNING:**
DAILY MEDITATIONS FOR WOMEN
Hazelton Meditations

+ **THE VERBALLY ABUSIVE RELATIONSHIP**
Patricia Evans

+ **STEP BACK: A STEPMOTHER'S HANDBOOK**
Margit Eva Bernard

Acknowledgments

I have so many to thank for their help, guidance and encouragement through the many years of shaping this memoir.

First, a brilliant young man, **Erik Lieberman,** so wise for his years, was the first to help me tackle the task of unraveling my complicated life and shaping it into book form.

Bruce Cook, a dear friend and an author, encouraged me to change the direction of my story. He named it *My Four Hollywood Husbands.*

Special appreciation goes to friends and early readers, **Susan Gillotti, Rachel Druten, Stephen Breimer and Kathy Strong.**

Thanks to my ever-patient editor, **Alaina Bixon,** who revised one draft after another and taught me much along the way. My gratitude for her utmost kindness and expertise.

Most of all, my heartfelt thanks and eternal love to **Roger,** Hollywood Husband Four, who read and reread this dyslexic's story, terrible spelling and all. What would I do without him!

About the Author

Joyce Bulifant's extensive credits on stage and on TV have made her a familiar face and popular personality. She played Gavin MacLeod's wife, Marie, on "The Mary Tyler Moore Show" and appeared in "Airplane," the Disney musical "The Happiest Millionaire," and many game shows, especially "The Match Game."

Under contract at Universal, she guest starred with Fred Astaire and on "The Virginian," "Destry Rides Again," and "Thriller," among others.

Her many TV credits include roles in "Perry Mason," "Gunsmoke," "My Three Sons," "Just Shoot Me," and "Weird Science." She has appeared in many theaters across the United States.

Ms. Bulifant has written and performed in two one-woman shows: "Life upon the Wicked Stage" and "Remembering Helen Hayes with Love." She also wrote an NBC movie of the week and wrote and directed "Gifts of Greatness" and "Different Heroes, Different Dreams."

Ms. Bulifant is Executive Vice President of The Dyslexia Foundation. She has served on many boards. With the help of the Mt. Sopris Rotary Club, she founded the River Bridge Regional Center, a Colorado advocacy organization for abused children.

Connect with Joyce at JoyceBulifant.com

CPSIA information can be obtained
at www.ICGtesting.com
Printed in the USA
BVOW03s1356300917

496375BV00001B/78/P